Notre-Dame

Also by Agnès Poirier

Touché: A Frenchwoman's Take on the English
Left Bank: Art, Passion and the Rebirth of Paris 1940–50

Notre-Dame

The Soul of France

Agnès Poirier

ONEWORLD

A Oneworld Book

First published by Oneworld Publications, 2020

Copyright © Agnès Poirier, 2020

ISBN 978-1-78607-799-8
eISBN 978-1-78607-800-1

Typeset by Hewer Text UK Ltd, Edinburgh
Map of central Paris copyright © Martin Lubikowski, ML Design, London
Printed and bound in Great Britain by Clays Ltd, Elcograf S.p.A.

Oneworld Publications
10 Bloomsbury Street, London, WC1B 3SR, United Kingdom
3754 Pleasant Ave, Suite 100, Minneapolis, MN 55409, USA

Stay up to date with the latest books,
special offers, and exclusive content from
Oneworld with our newsletter

Sign up on our website
oneworld-publications.com

MIX
Paper from
responsible sources
FSC® C018072

I have never felt anything like this before [. . .]
I have never seen anything so movingly serious and sombre.
Sigmund Freud, in a letter to his fiancée, Martha,
19 November 1885

It is not enough to look at Notre-Dame, one must live it.
At length. Daily. She would not be, for us, God's servant,
if she was not of any use to us too.
Paul Claudel, 1951

To *Ma Dame*,
Garance

Contents

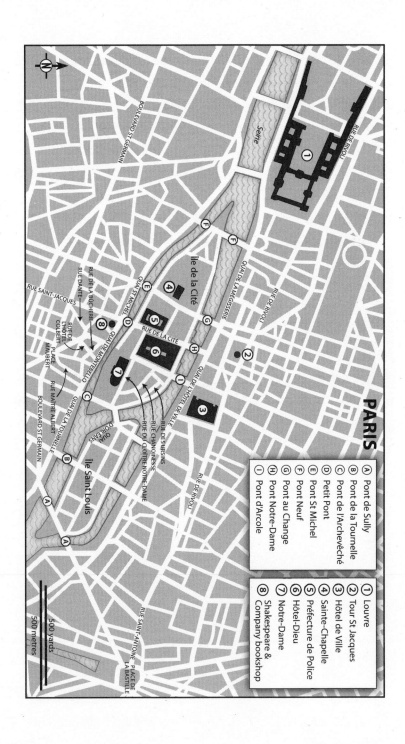

PARIS

Letter legend:
- (A) Pont de Sully
- (B) Pont de la Tournelle
- (C) Pont de l'Archevêché
- (D) Petit Pont
- (E) Pont St Michel
- (F) Pont Neuf
- (G) Pont au Change
- (H) Pont Notre-Dame
- (I) Pont d'Arcole

Number legend:
- (1) Louvre
- (2) Tour St Jacques
- (3) Hôtel de Ville
- (4) Sainte-Chapelle
- (5) Préfecture de Police
- (6) Hôtel-Dieu
- (7) Notre-Dame
- (8) Shakespeare & Company bookshop

500 metres
500 yards

Lateral view of Notre-Dame, after an engraving by M. Baldus.

Prologue

Of the night of the fire I remember a kaleidoscope of images, a collision of emotions, in quick succession. Seeing bright-yellow plumes of smoke through my kitchen window coiling into the sky, then rushing down the stairs onto quai de la Tournelle, standing right opposite Notre-Dame's south rose window, the red and orange tongues of fire leaping from the roof, the resounding silence of the crowd, the stunned look in people's eyes, the horrific beauty of the moment, tears pearling on cheeks, lips forming silent prayers, the precise, focused actions of fire-fighters as if suddenly transformed into field surgeons, fire hoses appearing at every corner like giant serpents, the flaming torch of the spire about to collapse, the pink-hued medieval stones against a royal-blue sky, then the black smoke rising from the north tower, and the unbearable realization and excruciating thought: Our Lady might go.

We need certainties: they are the framework of our existence, the signposts without which we can't navigate life, let alone endure its many tests and trials; for 850 years Notre-Dame was one such. Those of us who had forgotten received a shocking reminder on the night of 15 April 2019. If Notre-Dame could crumble in front of our eyes and disappear from our lives, so too could those other certainties – democracy, peace and fraternity. The head teachers of Paris, who summoned psychologists to assist in primary schools the morning after, understood this perfectly. Many children brought with them little plastic bags filled with fragments of blackened timber that they had picked up from balconies and pavements. Their parents had told them that those tiny bits of charcoal dated back to the Crusades, and they now needed to be comforted with the thought that nothing irreparable had taken place. Reassuring the children was easier than reassuring ourselves.

That evening, as the first images of the tragedy started flooding onto social networks and TV screens, a wave of emotion almost immediately surged towards the tiny island of Île de la Cité in Paris, the cradle of France, from every corner of the world. We Parisians felt, as often in history, at one with the world, united in a harmony of grief.

Why were we all feeling so traumatized?

Notre-Dame has always been far more than just a cathedral, a place of worship for Catholics and a beautiful monument whose stained glass dates back to the thirteenth century. Notre-Dame is one of mankind's greatest architectural achievements, the face of civilization and the soul of a nation. Both sacred and secular, Gothic and revolutionary, medieval and romantic, she has always offered a place of communion and refuge to everyone, whether believers or atheists, Christians or otherwise.

Victor Hugo and his hunchback transformed Notre-Dame into a world heroine and saved her from the dire neglect into which she had fallen 200 years ago. She rose again in the 1860s, in neo-medieval magnificence, thanks to the architect Eugène Viollet-le-Duc, a scholar of medieval art who reinvented Notre-Dame and gave her a spire with which she could have been born. Through the new art forms of photography and cinema she became a universal icon, a character of flesh and blood in the world's imagination, alongside Quasimodo, Esmeralda and the monstrous but endearing gargoyles adorning her façade. In this way a love of Notre-Dame, this living being of a Gothic cathedral, has passed from one generation to the next.

Her mesmerizing beauty also made the possibility of her demise all the more inconceivable. Built and rebuilt over ten centuries, a constant work of perfection in progress, Notre-Dame's loveliness is both unique and multi-faceted. Everyone has their favourite view of the cathedral. For some it is the view from pont de l'Archevêché, as one walks from the Left Bank towards the garden lying in the shadows of her flying buttresses, or slightly further to the east, from the middle of pont de la Tournelle, where the cathedral rises like the majestic prow of a ship called *France*. For others it is from quai d'Orléans on Paris's twin island, Île Saint-Louis, where she suddenly appears at the curve of the leafy embankment, or perhaps simply from the middle of the parvis – the square in front of the main doors of the cathedral,[1] the west rose window and twin towers in all their glory. For others still it is from quai Montebello and the terrace of the Shakespeare & Company bookshop.

Pablo Picasso liked the view from the garden at the back. On 15 May 1945, the bull-fighting enthusiast asked the photographer Brassaï: 'Have you ever photographed Notre-Dame from behind? I quite like Viollet-le-Duc's spire. It looks like a banderilla sticking out of her back!'[2]

My own favourite is from the corner of rue de la Bûcherie and rue de l'Hôtel Colbert, below quai de Montebello, at the bottom of three medieval steps, right next to the building where in October 1948 Simone de Beauvoir rented a tiny attic room with a view of the spire. At street level this narrow glimpse of Notre-Dame keeps you guessing and wanting to see more, and infallibly draws you towards her.

Notre-Dame's beauty is of a kind one never takes for granted; it is a constantly renewed miracle, which stuns you each time you meet her gaze. The secret of her loveliness lies in a powerful combination of familiarity and nobility, both warm and grandiose. How can a monument be so intimate and so imposing at the same time?

To dive into Notre-Dame's past is to immerse oneself in the soul of France, a history full of glory, torment and contradictions. In the last 850 years, Notre-Dame has witnessed the best of France and the worst of France. On 15 April 2019 she almost died as a result of human carelessness and was only saved *in extremis* by the courage of those ready to sacrifice their lives for her.

*

Notre-Dame: The Soul of France pays tribute to Maurice de Sully, the peasants' son who became bishop of Paris and oversaw the initial construction of the cathedral in the late twelfth century; and it features Henri IV, who, realizing that he couldn't govern against Paris, converted to Catholicism, paid his respects to Notre-Dame and reconciled a country deeply divided by thirty years of war between Protestants and Catholics. Henri's son, Louis XIII, consecrated his crown and France's fortune to the Virgin Mary at Notre-Dame, and his own son, Louis XIV, the Sun King, fulfilled his father's vow.

In 1789 and through Robespierre's Terror, the shrewd cathedral organist played revolutionary songs and the 'Marseillaise' instead of religious hymns, and an equally astute canon decided to safeguard the statues of the Sun King and his father, leaving the Virgin Mary to fend for herself alone before stern atheists and staunch republicans. He did well: they only dared remove her golden crown. The twenty-eight kings of the façade's upper gallery were less fortunate: each of them lost his head. Napoleon restored Notre-Dame, which had been rededicated as a temple of reason during the revolution, to her original faith. By choosing to be crowned emperor there in 1804 he also placed her at the centre of France's public and political life, paving the way for Victor Hugo and his hunchback.

Hugo's novel, written during the tumultuous days of the July Revolution of 1830, perfectly encapsulated the communion between the rebellious people of Paris, the cathedral's deformed bell-ringer Quasimodo and the beautiful bohemian Esmeralda, under the watchful gaze of Archdeacon Frollo. The success of the novel, published with richly evocative illustrations, was such that the whole country suddenly reappraised its medieval heritage and felt the need to attend to its crumbling monuments. Shortly after publication, France's national service for historic monuments was created and soon a new breed of architects, both artists and scholars, was recruited by the state to resurrect the past grandeur of old stones.

For twenty-two years Viollet-le-Duc painstakingly restored Notre-Dame to neo-medieval splendour. A few years after the spire was finished, Baron Haussmann extensively redesigned Paris and the Île de la Cité. By clearing medieval dwellings and demolishing narrow lanes nearby, Haussmann added majesty to the cathedral. Now standing alone on the tip of the island, she was visible from miles away.

On the night of the fire, many Parisians thought of 26 August 1944 when, having just walked down the Champs-Élysées acclaimed by two million of his compatriots, General de Gaulle stopped at Notre-Dame to attend a Te Deum, a special service celebrated with glorious music to give thanks following a time of peril. As he entered the packed cathedral through the central portal, gunshots rang out from the upper gallery. Snipers were shooting at the French leader, but de Gaulle kept walking, head high, into the nave towards the choir. The crowd had thrown themselves flat on the marble floor but, on seeing de Gaulle so calm and seemingly unaffected, they slowly resumed their places on the pews. The Magnificat was kept short and the general left as he came in, walking tall.

What would de Gaulle make of the battle over Notre-Dame's reconstruction? While the embers were still warm, French opinion seemed to divide into opposing groups, those wishing to see her as she was again and those wanting to add a touch of twenty-first-century genius. Will this be a battle between the timid and the daring, or between the wise and the foolish? Even the French prime minister, Édouard Philippe, couldn't help launching an international design competition for the rebuilding of the spire only two days after the fire. President Macron himself talked of rebuilding the cathedral to be 'even more beautiful than before' in just five years. Their words unleashed the most extravagant wave of ideas on social networks: among them, a crystal spire, a roof garden, a gigantic golden torch, a swimming-pool roof and a glass dome. Architects, desperately looking for publicity, embraced the international competition and promoted their fantastical plans for Notre-Dame. Pandora's box was open.

What is this French urge to be radical, to redesign, to reform and dazzle the world? Do we really think our twenty-first-century genius can match that of Notre-Dame's medieval builders'? Why not simply, for once, preserve and restore Notre-Dame to the state in which Viollet-le-Duc left her in 1865? There will still be an opportunity to reconfigure her surroundings and access for her fourteen million visitors a year, which were, at best, shambolic. There may even be a chance to create a long-desired and much-needed museum across the parvis, at the Hôtel-Dieu, a medieval hospital which is today partially empty.

The battle for the reconstruction of Notre-Dame has just begun and it promises to be fierce. The three richest families of France – the Pinaults, the Arnaults and the Bettencourts, who pledged 500 million euros for Notre-Dame's rebuilding as the fire was ravishing the roof – have had to justify their actions. Weren't they actually more interested in the tax breaks usually attached to such donations than in the fate of the cathedral, asked the Gilets Jaunes (Yellow Vests). Couldn't they spend that sort of money on people in need rather than old stones? Weren't there worthier causes than a great pile of charred debris?

Writing *Notre-Dame: The Soul of France* has been a singular journey, from a state of desolation to one of quiet optimism. Since 16 April 2019 when, as dawn broke in pink hues over the Seine, I saw Notre-Dame reappear, still standing, hurt yet magnificent, I have remained timidly hopeful. A few hours earlier, binoculars in hand, I had punched the air when I realized that her stained-glass windows had survived.

Meeting the men and women who saved Notre-Dame; talking to those who have tended to her like the most attentive nurses through the following weeks and months, 24/7, strengthening her structure, painstakingly collecting and storing every charred or broken remnant that can be reused; interviewing those who will advise on her reconstruction and those who will finance it; visiting the building site, touching the stone, strange as it sounds; even taking a blood test for lead poisoning – all this has made me acutely aware of the challenges that lie ahead and of the boundless and unconditional goodwill and commitment there is to see her rise again.

1

15 April 2019

The Night of the Fire

'That night, I died.'

Philippe Villeneuve

April in Paris.

The last few days have been blissful: unadulterated blue skies, chestnut and cherry trees in full blossom, an explosion of colours, bright yellow and pink waves rippling down from the heights of Montmartre to the leafy boulevards of Montparnasse, from the Tuileries Gardens at the bottom of the Champs-Élysées to the little park of Notre-Dame cathedral, where children from the neighbourhood love to play after school. This is Monday 15 April 2019, the beginning of Easter week, and those little Parisians are looking forward to their fortnight of spring holiday starting on Friday. That, and egg-hunting.

In the morning, the Cannes Film Festival unveiled the poster for its seventy-second season, taking place a month later. It is always an event. This year it features a young Agnès Varda, the French director who has recently died at the age of ninety. Perched on the back of a male technician, the 26-year-old gamine puts her eye to a camera set perilously high on a wooden platform while in the background the Mediterranean scintillates in the sun. The original black-and-white photograph from 1955 has been 'colourized' bright orange. It is a magnificent ode to cinema and to the wonderful director.

Paris is also bristling with expectation, of a political nature. Tonight at 8 p.m. the French president, Emmanuel Macron, will address the nation and hopefully put an end to the weeks of unrest unleashed by the Gilets Jaunes' polymorphous and radical protest. There have been twenty-two consecutive Saturdays of demonstrations throughout France, bringing havoc and destruction to some city centres, including Paris; and if the movement has by now mostly discredited itself through its casual violence and inability to express a coherent message, the French still want their president and his government to come up with proposals that will bring a sense of closure to the nation.

French political pundits and international correspondents have been trying to figure out what 'big' measures Emmanuel Macron might be about to announce, especially since he has already met most of the Gilets Jaunes' early demands – including the scrapping of fuel tax. One rumour circulates among political journalists: the president might choose to close down the ENA (École Nationale d'Administration), the famous elite school founded in 1945 by Charles de Gaulle to train the country's highest civil servants. This would indeed be momentous news. Conceived as a democratic recruitment system for the civil service through its exacting exams, the ENA has for a long time been synonymous with French meritocracy. Its students, for instance, never depend on their families to fund their education; instead, the state pays them a salary throughout their studies. However, over the years the school has been criticized for conditioning a *pensée unique* (one-track thinking), instilling in the future elite a rigid way of looking at the role of the state and the world.

On the Île de la Cité, one of the two small islands at the heart of the French capital, 'the head, the heart and the marrow of Paris',[1] as it was already known in the twelfth century, the cathedral's bells are about to ring for vespers. It is 5.45 p.m. and parents are gathering in front of the local primary school gates, waiting for their children to come out, sweaty and dishevelled. On place Maubert, a small square ensconced on boulevard Saint-Germain parallel to Notre-Dame's south rose window, the bakery Chez Isabelle, which scooped Paris's 'best croissant' and 'best apple tart' prizes the previous year, is well prepared for the imminent onslaught of little gourmands and their parents. The lucky ones will be granted a late *goûter* of *pain au chocolat* while their parents buy the evening baguette, preferably from the latest batch, still warm from the oven. Next door Laurent Dubois, master *fromager* (cheese-maker), is also ready. The pre-dinner buying rush is a well-known fixture of Parisian life. 'Have you bought the bread?', followed by 'Do we have any cheese?', are probably the sentences most commonly uttered in Paris every day between 6 p.m. and 8 p.m.

It has become a daily ritual: a dozen American tourists and their guide, who specializes in gastronomic tours of the French capital, have gathered in front of Laurent Dubois' round glass domes, which exhibit his latest cheese creations – quince Roquefort, calvados Camembert, walnut Brie, among others.

The group is given a mini-lecture on cheese before being invited to step into the shop for tasting and purchasing. Parisians have grown accustomed to living their daily lives among an ever-growing number of such visitors. Mass tourism has transformed many parts of Paris such as this one – place Maubert, the Left Bank and the vicinity of Notre-Dame – into what sometimes feels like a permanent beehive. It has its downside, of course, but Parisians and tourists share at least one thing: their love of Paris. A communion of spirit.

Inside Notre-Dame cathedral, a similar friendly co-existence prevails. On this Monday afternoon, while Canon Jean-Pierre Caveau, helped by the soprano Emmanuelle Campana and the organist Johann Vexo, leads vespers in the nave, hundreds of tourists wander quietly in the aisles and ambulatory. With fourteen million visitors in 2018, Notre-Dame is one of the most popular monuments in the world. Open every day of the year, free of charge, it offers two thousand Masses and celebrations annually.[2]

The countdown to Easter has started. The priest is reading Psalm 27:

> The Lord is my light and my salvation; whom shall I fear? The Lord is the strength of my life; of whom shall I be afraid?
>
> When the wicked, even mine enemies and my foes, came upon me to eat up my flesh, they stumbled and fell.
>
> Though an host should encamp me, my heart shall not fear; though war should rise against me, in this will I be confident.

At 6.18 p.m. a fire alarm rings and a message flashes on the cathedral security guard's computer screen: *Zone nef sacristie*

(Nave sacristy zone), except there is no fire in the sacristy, the small building on the south flank of the cathedral. The guard, who has only been doing the job for a couple of days and hasn't been told that the fire-alert messaging system is particularly arcane and that the zones are vague, naturally concludes it is a false alarm. There have been a few of them lately, especially since the beginning of important restoration work to the spire, which is now covered with a giant metallic lacework of scaffolding. At 6.42 p.m. a second fire alarm rings.

A few minutes later, Monsignor Benoist de Sinety, the vigorous and youthful-looking 50-year-old vicar-general of the archdiocese of Paris, leaves his residence on rue des Ursins, a medieval street near the cathedral once called rue d'Enfer (Hell Street), and jumps on his scooter. Heading towards the church of Notre-Dame-des-Champs on boulevard Montparnasse for an evening of prayers, Monsignor de Sinety zips through the narrow streets of the island encircling the cathedral, rue Chanoinesse, then rue du Cloître-Notre-Dame, and is about to cross the Seine at pont de l'Archevêché when he briefly looks in his side mirror. He slams on the brakes and turns his head towards Notre-Dame. Flames are leaping out of the cathedral's roof.[3]

*

The first call to the fire brigade is logged at 6.48 p.m., four minutes after the guard has finally been told that the fire-alert message indicates the cathedral's main attic, not the sacristy, and two minutes after he has climbed the 300 narrow steps and opened the door to the inferno already raging. The 'forest',

Notre-Dame's latticework roof structure of 1,300 oak beams, most of which date from the thirteenth century, is being consumed alive.

At the Élysée Palace, the president finishes recording his address to the nation while French TV channels are busy preparing special editions to comment on his announcements. Not for long. Pictures and videos taken by passers-by, first of black smoke coming out of the spire, then of orange and red tongues of fire licking at the sky, are proliferating on social networks.

Exactly 19 kilometres away Marie-Hélène Didier, a National Heritage curator in charge of France's religious art, and Laurent Prades, Notre-Dame's general manager, have just arrived in Versailles; they are attending the reopening of Madame de Maintenon's royal apartment at the palace. Franck Riester, France's culture minister, is also there. After three years of painstaking restoration work, the four beautiful rooms where Louis XIV's secret wife lived between 1680 and 1715 are about to open to the public. Champagne hasn't yet been served when mobile phones start vibrating in guests' pockets. Madame de Maintenon and Versailles will have to wait.[4]

With one hand fumbling in her bag for her car key, Marie-Hélène Didier immediately calls Philippe Villeneuve, a chief architect at Historic Monuments, one of thirty-nine responsible for France's architectural heritage, each of whom looks after a portfolio of important buildings. In 1893, the Department of Historic Monuments started recruiting the most gifted art historians and architects of their generation through a series of thorough and demanding tests.[5] 'To keep a historic monument alive in our present times requires erudition, talent, respect, discretion and moral qualities.'[6] They are France's elite architectural corps.

Notre-Dame belongs to Philippe Villeneuve. Or rather, Philippe Villeneuve belongs to Notre-Dame. As a small boy with a passion for organ music, he found his vocation in architecture while seated on the wooden benches of the cathedral, listening for hours to Pierre Cochereau, Notre-Dame's legendary organist,[7] improvising on one of the world's largest organs, with 5 manuals, 111 stops and 7,374 pipes.[8]

Philippe Villeneuve is in the Charentes region, in the southwest of France, and is already driving at 180 km/h to the nearest train station, La Rochelle.[9] Marie-Hélène Didier, now too in her car, has clearly made the wrong decision. She is soon stuck in traffic on Paris's Right Bank, between the Louvre and the Hôtel de Ville, and all she can do is switch off both the radio and Twitter and watch, feeling completely powerless. Notre-Dame is in flames right in front of her.

Fortunately, Laurent Prades has opted for public transport and hopped on the RER, the regional line to Paris from Versailles. The fastest train takes fifty-eight minutes. Saint-Michel-Notre-Dame station has just been closed, though, and he must exit at Musée d'Orsay. He will have to finish his journey by bike: luckily he owns a pass for the Vélib' public cycle-sharing scheme which allows him to use any of the freely available bicycles found at docks on every Paris street corner. He will then need to get through police lines as fast as he can. As general manager of the cathedral he is not only in charge of its sixty employees but he also knows where the keys are – all 100 of them. He knows every code too, including those of

Notre-Dame's treasury and another discreet safe placed in the chapel called Notre-Dame des Sept Douleurs (Mater Dolorosa), at the far end of the cathedral, right behind the apse. In this double-bulletproof-glass safe lies the crown of thorns. Cycling towards the cathedral under a rain of ashes and fiery flakes, the 42-year-old Laurent Prades has one obsession: to save the Catholic world's most precious religious relic from destruction.

*

'The guilt,' says Jean-Claude Gallet, three-star general, veteran of Afghanistan and commander-in-chief of the Paris fire brigade, 'the guilt is overwhelming. How could we have arrived when the fire had already spread so dramatically? Did our switchboard miss a call?'[10] In fact, the firemen haven't failed and haven't missed any calls. And it takes them only a few minutes to arrive after the first call, but it does indeed already appear too late to save Notre-Dame's 800-year-old roof.

General Gallet knows about fire, all kinds of fire. After graduating from the elite military school of Saint-Cyr, he enrolled in the Paris fire brigade. Napoleon established the fire brigade in 1811, after narrowly escaping an arson attack at an Austrian embassy ball in Paris. He wanted fire-fighting to become professional and efficient, and created the first military unit of fire-fighters, whose members were the sappers of the Imperial Guard. To this day, the battalion remains dedicated to safeguarding Paris.[11] Its motto is 'Save or perish'.

Paris firemen and -women[12] are not only soldiers: they enjoy unique training and skills. Compared with fire departments in other big cities such as London and New York, they stand out. For a start they are young, with an average age of twenty-seven (that of fire-fighters in other capital cities is over forty). Of small to medium height, they are wiry and strong, and are subjected to a daily routine of strenuous physical exercises. Among them is the 'plank',[13] which they need to perform twice a day, fully dressed with uniform and helmet on. Fire-fighters need to be able to hoist themselves up onto a small plank, placed at a height of 2.40 metres, with a simple pull-up; the test, introduced in 1895, is designed to make sure they can escape after floors have collapsed under them. If they fail they can't go out on missions and must get back into shape before they do. At fifty-four General Gallet is still regularly doing the 'plank', just not twice daily. General Gallet calls Paris firemen and -women 'gymnasts', and this is one of the reasons why, unlike in other capital cities, they choose to attack fires from within buildings, not from the outside.

When General Gallet arrives on the parvis of Notre-Dame with his men, among them Lieutenant-Colonel Gabriel Plus and General Jean-Marie Gontier, his second-in-command, he knows he can tear up the rulebook. It is already too late to save the roof and there is a limit to the quantity of water you can force on medieval stones. As for the thirteenth-century rose windows, the water pressure would simply pulverize them back into sand. Gallet must think differently, and fast.

His plan is to attack the fire on all fronts at once. He sends vanguards of fighters up the narrow spiral staircase to the cornice, 44 metres high, to try and circumvent the fire from the side; he sets up a north–south cross-curtain of water between the roof and the towers in order to cool down the atmosphere and protect the belfries, which together harbour ten giant bronze bells; he asks for Colossus, the brigade's robot, a half-tonne terrestrial drone equipped with a powerful hose firing a jet of water at 3,000 litres per minute, to be ready to enter the nave and prevent falling debris from starting a fire in the choir and transepts. He knows that at some point soon his firefighters won't be able to withstand the heat and the rain of burning molten lead inside the nave.

*

Adrien Goetz has just finished giving a lecture at the Sorbonne on the importance of Jacques-Louis David's painting *The Coronation of Napoleon*. The elegantly dressed 54-year-old art historian and Victor Hugo connoisseur is clearing his desk when a news alert on his smartphone warns him of the dramatic events taking place a few streets away. Clutching his briefcase under his arm, he walks as fast as he can towards the Seine.[14] As he turns into place Maubert a picture of the cathedral spire in flames pops up on his phone's screen. He can see huge, brown-yellow plumes of smoke billowing into the sky above him. To steady his nerves, he remembers what he has told his students: the reason why we all remember the coronation of Napoleon, in Notre-Dame in 1804, is because the event became a painting, an image. Images make history.

From place Maubert Adrien Goetz dives down rue Maître-Albert, a serpentine little medieval street left untouched by Baron Haussmann and which bore the name of rue Perdue

(Lost Street) until the mid-nineteenth century. 'Then I stop in my tracks. I am here.'[15] What strikes him first is the acrid smell of charcoal, and what soon terrifies him is the changing wind. The distinct sound of timber cracking fills the air. On quai de la Tournelle, where he now stands, throngs of people, Parisians like him and tourists, are standing side by side, their faces all turned towards Notre-Dame. Despite the crowd, the silence on the riverbanks is deafening. Until 7.57 p.m.

'The spire! No!' From the crowd, a scream – the single word *Non!* – ascends into the sky of Paris as the 750-tonne spire wrought of heavy oak and lead crashes down, breaking the stone vault of the nave. 'I will have lived through this. I will have seen the spire of Notre-Dame fall with my own eyes,'[16] thinks the historian. Next to him an old man weeps. He is not alone.

Standing at the command post set up in front of the cathedral, the fire brigade's spokesperson, Lieutenant-Colonel Plus, doesn't see the spire fall. He only hears it. As he instinctively turns his eyes towards the façade, the blast forces open all the cathedral doors at once, each of which weighs several tonnes.[17]

Everybody's pulse now beats even faster, whether fire-fighters combating the blaze or bystanders positioned, immobile, on both banks of the Seine; whether Parisians, French or foreigners, near or far away, in front of their TVs or their mobile-phone screens. Millions and millions of people around the world are now joined in communion, in fear and in dread.

Events seem to accelerate. It is just after 8 p.m. The president and his wife Brigitte have arrived. The televised address has been cancelled. Notre-Dame is the only thing France now cares about. At the police prefecture across the cathedral square, a ground-floor conference room has been transformed into a war room. Most of the government, from the prime minister to the minister of culture, are there, along with the prefect of police, the president of the National Assembly, the public prosecutor, the mayor, Anne Hidalgo, the archbishop of Paris, Monsignor Michel Aupetit, his vicar-general, Benoist de Sinety and the cathedral rector, Monsignor Patrick Chauvet. They are anxiously waiting for General Gallet to brief them on the situation.

Laurent Prades has finally reached the cathedral after leaving his bike lying on the pavement and crossing two police lines, waving his ID. He arrives almost at the same time as the fire brigade's chaplain, Jean-Marc Fournier, also a veteran of Afghanistan. Marie-Hélène Didier is now only fifteen minutes away. Many other National Heritage curators and chief architects from Historic Monuments have converged on the Île de la Cité too, to help. On seeing their IDs, the police have let them all in. In France, art and history command respect.

They all have only one thing in mind: to save Notre-Dame's treasury and as many of the thousands of religious relics, art objects and historic paintings present in the cathedral as possible. Equipped with gleaming fire helmets, this battalion of historians divides up into two groups. One, accompanied by fire-fighters, will collect the art, whether in the treasury next to the sacristy or deep inside the cathedral, while the other forms a human chain leading from the sacristy to the garden at the foot of the flying buttresses. There the prefabs put in place for the restoration work will provide a temporary warehouse for all the art objects under the watchful gaze of the BRI,[18] the elite police research and intervention unit, who are armed to the teeth.

In the sacristy, with water up to her calves, Marie-Hélène Didier goes straight to the wooden cabinet where the tunic of Saint Louis hangs. King Louis IX, known as Saint Louis since his canonization in 1297, was said to have been wearing this simple white linen garment when he brought Jesus' crown of thorns to Paris from Byzantium in 1239, having paid a fortune for it.[19] Marie-Hélène also reaches for Saint Louis's scourge. A devout Catholic, the French king had a penchant for self-flagellation. Her colleagues go from one display window to another, breaking glass or forcing locks whenever necessary.

Laurent Prades and Chaplain Fournier are much closer to the blaze. They are deep inside the cathedral, behind the apse, in the chapel of Notre-Dame des Sept Douleurs. The nave is littered with burnt beams, just like giant black spillikins; a patch of dark-blue sky can be seen through a large hole in the roof; firebrands are flying in the suffocating, smoke-filled air. Prades tells himself that he must stop looking at the devastation around him; he must focus on the task ahead.[20] In his absence fire-fighters have tried to force the double safe open, but to no avail. Now armed with the right key, Prades needs to remember the right code. He tries one – a message of error flashes. And another. His memory is failing him. If phone calls can't get through, text messages, however, work. Two sacristans know the code. He asks them for help. At 8.42 p.m. he receives a text message with the right code.[21] The door opens. The men retrieve the red leather casket containing the crown of thorns and also a nail from the holy cross and a piece of the cross itself. They retreat to the sacristy under a hail of embers and molten lead. Chaplain Fournier can't stop thinking of the Italian fireman

Mario Trematore, who, on 11 April 1997, saved Christ's shroud from the flames as a devastating fire engulfed the Guarini chapel in Turin. Trematore had managed, single-handedly and with only the help of a hatchet, to smash his way through a bullet-proof shield and snatch the silver casket holding the shroud.[22]

The mayor's office has organized trucks to come and transport the precious relics and works of art to the town hall, just across the Seine, on the Right Bank; the mayor has safe rooms where they can stay until they are despatched to the Louvre. Marie-Hélène Didier gets into the first truck to leave, next to the driver, the crown of thorns and Saint Louis' tunic on her lap. Across the square, where news of the art rescue operation has reached the war room, timid smiles light up faces. The respite doesn't last.

The police have sent drones to hover high above Notre-Dame. The aim is to survey the fire and visually inspect the damage done to the building's structure. A big screen now relays what the drones see. Viewers, staring wide-eyed, put their hands over their mouths. Terrifying images of a giant burning crimson cross, covering the nave and transepts like a kind of sorcerers' Sabbath, strike everyone to the core. For some, the shock is too violent. Rector Chauvet faints in the mayor's arms.[23] However, worse is yet to come.

One of the fire-fighters, Laurent Clerjeau, is also a professional sketch artist. He has been feeding generals Gallet and Gontier with drawings for the last hour or so. His task is to give the high command a *vue d'ensemble*, an overall idea of the fire's nature and progression, of changes in wind direction, of all the details which may help them combat it. He regularly asks permission to go all over the cathedral in order to get a clearer idea of the fast-developing situation. Equipped only with a pencil and a notepad, he can move fast and report back immediately. Just after 8 p.m. he asks to go up to the chimaera gallery, which links the two towers. Something has been nagging him for some time. What was the dim glow showing at a small window in the north belfry? He has also noticed that the belfry's *abat-sons*, or louvre boards, are slightly ajar. This is worrying. Any opening in a burning building can create a suction effect and ignite smouldering fires. Besides, the southerly wind is now pushing the 800°C gas clouds created by the blaze directly towards the north tower. He runs up the 380 steps to the façade's upper gallery; the temperature is almost unbearable. Clerjeau quickly walks round the north tower and notices a semi-hidden door, probably opening onto a small staircase leading to the top. He breaks the lock with a few kicks and enters.[24] He looks up and instantly reaches for his radio: 'Fire in progress in the north tower!' On hearing those words at the command post 43 metres below, General Gallet turns pale.

The north tower houses eight massive bells, arranged in pairs over two levels, two pairs per floor. The whole structure sustaining them is made of very large and heavy wooden beams dating back to the Middle Ages, just like in the cathedral's attic. The bells have beautiful names: Gabriel, Anne-Geneviève, Denis, Marcel, Etienne, Benoît-Joseph, Maurice and Jean-Marie, and together they weigh 16.6 tonnes.

Should the wooden framework go up in flames the bells would come tumbling down, and with them the whole tower would collapse. The south tower, sheltering the cathedral's two other and biggest bells, the 13.2-tonne bourdon Emmanuel and

6-tonne Marie, would no doubt follow, and with the second tower crashing down so too would the whole façade and, in time, the rest of the building. Repercussions on the nearby buildings all around the cathedral, luckily by now mostly evacuated, would be inevitable.[25]

General Gallet quickly confers with his men, exchanges a few words. No need to say much: the eyes say it all. He has known every one of them for years; this makes decisions and communication easier and swifter. He now needs to submit his plan to the president. Time is of the essence. Gallet enters the war room in his fire-fighter's uniform, dripping with water. 'I needed to be brief and choose my words carefully,'[26] he would recall three months later.

The way he sees it is simple. The situation is so grave that audacity is the only option. Fifty men from the Groupe de reconnaissance et d'intervention en milieu périlleux (GRIMP), an elite intervention unit specializing in operations in perilous environments, are needed on the towers immediately to attack the fire close up, in hand-to-hand combat. 'If we want to see the towers still standing as dawn breaks tomorrow, this is our only chance.' A voice in the room breaks the heavy silence and asks: 'Have you assessed the risk?' General Gallet replies: 'The risk is consented to and accepted.' President Macron, his wife Brigitte close by, walks up to him and firmly grabs his arm. 'Thank you, general, go ahead, this is all very clear.'

While the GRIMP squad rushes up the spiral staircase to the platform separating the two towers and places grapplers, tethers and ropes in case of an emergency evacuation down the façade, another team has brought up additional hoses directly plugged into fire engines below. They will need as much water pressure as the hoses can muster.

A vanguard of fire-fighters is about to enter the north tower. Some look around them: on one side, the cathedral's roof, a cauldron from hell; on the other, 43 metres below, hundreds of fire-fighters gazing up at them, and on the bridges and riverbanks a sea of people, old and young, children in mothers' arms, of all colours and creeds, their faces turned towards them.

The north tower is now an inferno, with flames ten metres high. The floor separating the two sets of bells is ablaze. They will have to crawl up. The leading lieutenant tests every stair carefully, closely followed by his men. He hasn't seen the bells yet when one step, already burnt by the fire, gives way under his weight. His fall into the belfry is almost immediately stopped by his air tank.[27] After a few seconds of recuperation, he hauls himself up and continues his ascent.

The next thirty minutes will decide the fate of Notre-Dame.

General Gallet has also sent three men to the south tower to cool it down, and to prevent the flames spreading. They point their hoses towards Emmanuel and its sister, Marie. Emmanuel has been hanging here since 1686 and is one of the world's largest bells. Its deep voice, in F sharp, is only heard on rare occasions and shakes everyone present. As the water ripples down Emmanuel's waist, a lament starts reverberating throughout the tower. What is this? wonder the three fire-fighters. The bells are wailing and whimpering. Notre-Dame is weeping.[28]

It is 9.35 p.m. General Gallet steps forward in front of the TV cameras, alone. Someone has to let the French know of the seriousness of the situation. 'We don't know whether we will be able to sav— to stop the progress of the fire to the north belfry. If it collapses, I leave you to imagine the severity of the damage.' The millions of people watching him suddenly realize, at this precise moment, the mortal danger Our Lady is in. General Gallet chooses to ignore the deluge of questions that follow his statement, he has said enough. Back to the command post to be with his men.

As if on cue, Archbishop Aupetit sends a message on Twitter: 'To all the priests of Paris: the firemen are currently still fighting to save the towers of Notre-Dame. The timberwork, roof and spire have been destroyed. Let us pray. Ring your bells and spread the word.'

Adrien Goetz, among the crowd below massed on quai Montebello, instinctively knows how dramatic the moment is. For anyone able to see the towers, it is obvious we have reached a critical stage. Thousands and thousands of people are now filling rue Dante and rue de la Bûcherie, one of the Left Bank's oldest streets, dating back to the early thirteenth century, where traders sold logs. From there you can see part of the façade of the cathedral and the south flank with its rose window.

Events reminiscent of another age are now taking place on quai Saint-Michel: young and not-so-young Parisians have fallen on their knees. When was Paris last the setting for such stupefying scenes? Some are silently praying, while others are quietly singing Ave Marias. Those images, relayed on TV, stun this staunchly secular country, this viscerally sceptical people, and touch them to the core. Awestruck, France realizes how profoundly Christian its history is, even if it is buried under a century or more of secularism.

Then bells start chiming from every corner of the French capital, in fact from all over France, joining in an immense prayer for Notre-Dame. Priests have heard their archbishop's call. All the church bells of France are ringing for their siblings, prisoners of a deadly inferno. The moment is solemn; it is sublime.

General Gallet has ordered all his men out of the cathedral and sent Colossus, the robot, inside the blaze, into the nave. Only the fifty members of the GRIMP squad remain in the towers in close combat with the fire. He has also asked for laser range-finders to be placed around and inside Notre-Dame to constantly monitor the stability of the cathedral's structure. The laser data are not good: the cathedral is suffering greatly; its equilibrium is under terrible stress. 'I receive the news that the north gable has swayed one centimetre. One centimetre!'[29] General Gallet later confides. A building is deemed on the verge of collapsing if it sways just 2–3 millimetres.

General Gallet looks up at his men battling the fire in the north tower and on the upper gallery. 'From where I stand, the lights on their helmets make them look like fireflies.' He can't help thinking about his American friend, Joe Pfeifer, the first fire chief on the scene after the World Trade Center attack on the morning of 11 September 2001. The two men have spoken at a conference on leadership at Harvard. 'To go in or not to go in?' is always the question.

Notre-Dame feels different from anything he has lived through. 'She is a living being,' says General Gallet. Tonight, both a semantic and a paradigm shift are occurring at the heart of Paris. 'Notre-Dame was, for me, history, literature, iconography. She has now become stone and wood,'[30] realizes Adrien

Goetz while staring at her. The urge to say 'she' whenever referring to or simply thinking about Notre-Dame is slowly and organically imposing itself. We thought she was immortal, we thought she was made of imperishable matter, we thought she would bury Paris, she would see the end of times, long after we had all turned to ashes. It is not even a question of faith or belief, a question of being Catholic, Parisian or French. Anyone who has ever approached Notre-Dame and been touched by her beauty and benevolent presence realizes tonight how vulnerable she is.

Just as consecrated bread and wine become the body and the blood of Christ for Catholics, another kind of transubstantiation is taking place on the Île de la Cité and in the hearts and minds of onlookers, near and far. Notre-Dame is in fact made of flesh, she is a part of who we are.

It is 11 p.m. when General Gallet feels confident enough to announce to the president that the fire in the north tower has now been brought under control. Long minutes are necessary for the people present in the war room to absorb the extraordinary news, for which they had not dared to hope but had so fervently prayed.

At 11.30 p.m. President Macron, flanked by the prime minister, Édouard Philippe, and Mayor Hidalgo on his right, and the president of the National Assembly, the archbishop of Paris and General Gallet on his left, walks towards the TV cameras in front of Notre-Dame. He addresses the nation:

What has happened tonight is a terrible tragedy and I would like first of all like to salute the 500 firemen who have fought and are still fighting the fire with extreme courage and great professionalism and whose chief has proved extremely determined. I want to convey to them the gratitude of the whole nation. The worst has been avoided even if the battle has not yet been won. Difficult hours lie ahead of us but, thanks to their courage, the façade and the two towers have not collapsed.

The president almost whispers this last sentence. He continues:

I think of the Catholics, in France and in the world, I know how you feel, we are with you. I think of all Parisians and I think of all our compatriots, for Notre-Dame is our history, our literature, our collective imagination, the place where we have lived all our great moments, our wars and our liberations. It is the epicentre of our life, the kilometre zero of France; it is so many books, so many paintings, it is the cathedral of all the French people, even those who have never set foot in it. Her story is our story and she is burning. I feel the sadness, this inner shiver and dread we have all felt, but I also want us to feel hopeful.

He now smiles, almost energized:

There is hope in the pride of seeing all those who fought so hard to avoid the worst, the pride of knowing that 850 years ago we built this cathedral. I am now telling you, solemnly, that we will rebuild her, all of us together. It is our destiny. In a few hours, we will launch a public fund, we will ask the greatest talents to contribute to her reconstruction, for we will rebuild her, we will rebuild Notre-Dame. Because this is what the French expect, this is what our history deserves, because this is our profound destiny.[31]

*

The structure has been saved. Whether at home or on the banks of the River Seine, a whole nation is feeling punch-drunk. 'Little by little, the people in the crowd start talking to each other. We all look like survivors of a shipwreck.'[32] Adrien Goetz, like many others, will stay for a few hours more, until dawn, and keep vigil.

The hundreds of rescued art objects, relics and paintings have now all been stored in the town hall, from where the mayor has just rushed back. It is after midnight. Marie-Hélène Didier will later recall not feeling a thing when she had the saintly relics on her lap in the first truck to leave the cathedral.[33] Action had anaesthetized her emotions. But finally, in the secure environment of the town hall, in front of all the treasures now stored safely, the dam of emotions has burst and she can't hold back the tears. A torrent of tears. The thought that all could have perished is simply unbearable to contemplate.

*

'Shall we go inside?' asks President Macron, after his improvised address to the nation in front of Notre-Dame. General Gallet nods his consent. Standing in the cathedral's entrance, the president and his small entourage are greeted by a vision. Beyond the nave and the choir, filled with grey water and a huge pile of charred debris and blackened oak beams, the golden cross and the Pietà are still standing, immaculate. The Virgin Mary and the Christ lying in her arms appear in their pristine white marble, spared, untouched. To the right of this early seventeenth-century Pietà, by Nicolas Coustou, stands a marble statue of Louis XIII on his knees, offering his crown to the Virgin Mary, while on the left a statue of his son, Louis XIV, is looking at the mother of Christ with reverence and adoration. The spire and the vault have collapsed at their feet.

It is 2 a.m. when General Gallet makes another inspection of the cathedral. There are still six contained fires here and there, and it will take a couple of days to extinguish them all. 'Inside the nave, out of the corner of my eye, I see a white patch among the charred debris lying on what remains of the altar.' It is in fact a large beige leather-bound book, open, its pages covered with thick dust. 'As I get closer, intrigued, I can make out a word through the dust: *espérance* [hope].'[34] The lectionary, a collection of scripture readings, has survived the destruction. It is open on the hope of resurrection.

2

1163

The First Stone

'If this monument is one day finished, no other will ever compare.'

Robert de Thorigny[1]

I n the middle of the twelfth century, Paris was a capital city on the cusp of a phenomenal economic, political, territorial, intellectual and artistic expansion. It was about to enter 150 years of continuous growth and development of the kind it wouldn't see again, to this day. And it was during this most auspicious time that Notre-Dame cathedral was built.[2]

Despite the renaissance of cities between the tenth and the thirteenth centuries, only fifteen percent of the population were city-dwellers. Towns were therefore of a modest size: Marseilles had 10,000 inhabitants, Lyons 20,000. In fact, the most populous European cities could be found in Flanders and Italy: Ghent had 64,000 inhabitants, Florence 100,000 and both Milan and Venice, beacons of Christendom, as many as 200,000, compared to just 40,000 in London.

However, Paris achieved the feat of being by far the most populated city in the Western world, even in a kingdom that was mostly rural. With 270,000 inhabitants[3] living in a space of less than 400 hectares,[4] it was the city incarnate.

Paris was the capital of France, but what was France? At the end of the twelfth century the French royal domain was the shape of a *bandelette*, a narrow strip of the lushest farmland extending from the northern town of Amiens to Bourges in the south, with Paris at its epicentre. However, after a series of wars of conquest, by 1204 King Philip II, also known as Philip Augustus, had acquired for France a multitude of new territories: Normandy, Maine, Anjou, Touraine, Poitou and the rest of the Plantagenet lands down to the south-western town of Bordeaux on the Atlantic coast. In 1229 the Languedoc was ceded to the Count of Toulouse, who was a vassal to the king, while in 1285 Champagne was bought by royal decree. A few years later, Lyons and its surrounding area increased the size of France further.[5]

While other European cities usually fulfilled one or two functions (Ghent was an industrial centre, Bologna a university town, Venice a commercial power), Paris represented them all. First, it had a thriving economic life thanks to its many specialized artisans. In 1268 *Le Livre des métiers*, kept by the provost of Paris, Étienne Boileau, registered 900 different kinds of professional activity.[6] The very powerful drapers' trade, for instance, employed an army of skilled workers: wool-shearers, combers, carders, spinners, weavers, dyers and of course drapers themselves. And if you worked in wool you were not allowed to touch cotton or silk, two other trades that were as closely regulated.

Traders and merchants, especially in wheat, wine and wool, formed a particularly powerful group which held a monopoly on commerce using the River Seine.

Both royal and episcopal powers understood very quickly that they should work closely with those rich bourgeois.[7] Most of the manorial lords decided at this time to shift their place of residence to the city, where the products of their estates converged; merchants would then sell them on behalf of the lords. In a time of territorial conquests and economic growth, they all had an interest in joining forces. When he left for the Third Crusade in 1190,[8] Philip II pointedly chose to delegate the collection of royal taxes in his absence to seven such rich Parisian bourgeois, not to aristocratic relatives. Ten years later, Philip recruited more of them to help with both the administration and financial management of his recent territorial conquests, among them Normandy and the Languedoc. Thanks to their shrewd intendancy, those annexations doubled the royal fortune and made France the wealthiest kingdom in Europe.[9]

An economic powerhouse, with a skilful bourgeoisie at its heart growing ever more prosperous, Paris was also a religious centre, the seat of the diocese. On the Île de la Cité the all-powerful bishops of Paris lived in the episcopal palace, with hundreds of priests and canons to assist them in their duties. One of those was education. Paris quickly became renowned as a European centre of excellence with its prestigious episcopal schools and newly established universities. Throngs of young clerks and students flocked from the provinces of Normandy and Picardy and neighbouring regions such as England, Scandinavia, the Germanic lands, Flanders and Italy to the Île de la Cité to acquire an education. The poorest went to live south of the Seine, on what was not yet known as the Left Bank, where they could get cheaper rents. This student contingent, young, boisterous and male, represented ten percent of Paris's population, as compared with only two percent in the rest of the country. Prostitution was therefore tolerated, in order to protect the young women of the bourgeoisie from such a demographic imbalance and promiscuity. Paris didn't boast municipal brothels, but prostitutes could be found in any good tavern.

These students did not live secluded from the world. They were part of the times they lived in. Nearly all belonged to the Church; they were tonsured clerics, subject to the bishop's jurisdiction. Learning was a religious act but the mission for which their education was preparing them was an active one, and a secular, pastoral one. It was a verbal mission. They were to spread the Word – the knowledge of God – among the laymen.[10]

The ranks of students were very mobile and either swelled or melted away, depending on the quality of the master concerned. By 1150 Paris had overtaken Laon, Chartres and Saint-Denis. Its victory owed much to the glory that graced Abelard, the most brilliant teacher of his day. Bolder, more independent-minded masters – whose audacity attracted greater numbers of students – rented stalls on rue du Fouarre and the Petit Pont, both a stone's throw from the future cathedral. South of the Seine a whole new district, devoted entirely to study, was growing opposite the Île de la Cité.

Finally, Paris had regained its former status as the kingdom's capital city, originally bestowed by Clovis, the founder of the Merovingian dynasty, in the late fifth century. When Philip II gave it a strong, enclosing wall in 1190, capable of defending the royal treasury and the royal archives, which he had recently moved there, Paris officially imposed itself as the royal residence of choice. 'Paris was the king's city, the first city in medieval Europe to become what Rome had long since ceased to be: a genuine capital. Paris became the capital not of an empire, not of a certain Christendom, but of a kingdom, of *the* kingdom.'[11]

Little by little, Paris acquired a fourfold vocation: as the royal city, the merchant city, the bishop's city and the university city. 'In the narrow lanes where the schools sprang up a new spirit was born.'[12]

*

One has to immerse oneself in the daily life of the Île de la Cité from 1150 to 1300 to understand the extraordinary achievement that was the construction of Notre-Dame on the site of an already existing and functioning cathedral, which had just been renovated. The Île de la Cité, with its 15,000 inhabitants (compared to barely 1,000 today), was not just bustling with people; it was crowded with small dwellings separated only by very narrow streets in the middle of which lay both rubbish and excrement. The rich and the destitute lived alongside each other, and larger houses stood next to decrepit lodgings. The square outside the ancient cathedral was filled with the bric-à-brac of shops and stalls, the cries of street sellers and the pungent smells of fish or meat cut, boned and sold on open-air blocks. Fairs and markets were regular features, the two most popular events being, on 8 September, the onion and flower market, and roughly six months later, on the last day of Lent, the colourful ham fair, which sometimes required the chapter bailiff to intervene:

> In this parvis where one can contemplate
> the face of a superb temple
> A forest of hams grow from all sides
> as if they had been planted.[13]

Religious processions took place very regularly too, for instance whenever natural catastrophes occurred, such as floods or heavy rains. In this case, the shrine of Saint Genevieve, patron saint of Paris, was exhibited for everyone to see and supplicate to.

The square in front of the ancient cathedral was a theatre in all the meanings of the term. From the permanent gibbet sometimes hung a criminal sentenced to death by the bishop, who had judicial authority on his patch of land. Sometimes a platform was raised so that the *mystères* (mystery plays), could be performed.

*

Who financed the construction of Notre-Dame de Paris and, more generally, the whole urban redesign of the Île de la Cité? The short answer is that nobody knows for certain. Only a handful of accounting documents survive. Historians interested in the question went hunting for traces of donations for the construction and decoration of the cathedral by studying the chartularies and obituaries of independent archives,[14] and drew their conclusions from them.

It appears that everyone, from poor Parisians up to the king and his entourage, made donations for the construction of Notre-Dame or contributed to it in one way or another throughout the twelfth and thirteenth centuries. However, the bulk of the money seems to have come from one man, Bishop Maurice de Sully, through his large episcopal incomes, which he appears to have used almost entirely for this huge urban project. Those incomes were vast. The bishops owned the best land in a 50-kilometre radius around the Île de la Cité, and their enormous granaries were filled to the rafters with the tithes payable on every harvest. They also controlled the city, exploiting its markets and fairs and collecting many kinds of taxes, such as that imposed on every transaction done in Les Halles, already its trading centre and principal market.[15] Hence they profited directly from both the land and trade. More funds for Notre-Dame's construction could also be raised quickly by the sale of some of the diocese's properties: after all, it owned two-thirds of the whole Parisian real estate.

According to the monk Anchin, well known at the time for his chronicles, Maurice de Sully used 'his own funds rather than those of others'.[16] The son of peasants, Sully had no personal wealth and it was only through careful and astute management of his episcopal incomes that he could raise the necessary sums to finance his architectural projects.

Evidence of Sully's dedication and generosity is shown, in his will, by the large donation of 1,000 livres to pay for the lead for the new cathedral's roof.[17] Interestingly, two of his successors also proved most generous: Jean de Paris and Simon Matifas de Buci, the bishops who supervised the end of the construction and some reconstruction in the early fourteenth century. In his will in 1270, Jean de Paris left enough money to cover the final work on the transepts,[18] while Simón Matifas de Buci invested more than 5,000 livres between 1298 and 1304 in the creation of three axial chapels.[19]

Donations could take many forms: for instance, the establishment of chantries, or trust funds to employ priests to sing Masses for the souls of the recently departed, sometimes the donors themselves. Many rich bourgeois working for the French king, like Jean Sarrazin, Louis IX's chamberlain, set up numerous generous chantries at different Parisian churches and at Notre-Dame.[20] When chapels were built inside the cathedral, the bourgeois of Paris not only funded the creation of thirty-six chantries, one per chapel, but largely funded the building of each of those chapels.[21] Of course, the donations hardly covered the cost of the construction of the building itself; however, their existence shows that, as Sully had urged them to in his sermons,[22] the Parisian bourgeois must have contributed hard cash towards it – as an investment both in their felicity on earth and, more pointedly, in the peace of their souls after death. They had benefited so much from the continuous economic growth that they could lavishly donate to their new cathedral and also to other churches in Paris.[23] 'Rich laymen always made large donations because they were concerned about their souls,' wrote the French historian Georges Duby.[24]

The poorest also contributed significantly to the construction of Notre-Dame, not exactly willingly, but through hardship and making sacrifices. The 2,000 serfs who worked the bishop's lands had to pay the *taille* (land tax) levied on them by the

Church whenever it pleased. Between 1210 and 1232, that is to say at the time of the construction of Notre-Dame's façade, the serfs were forced to pay the *taille* five times, every four and a half years. The pressure was such that some dissident canons, fearing what they saw as a legitimate revolt, demanded that the serfs be exempted for the next twenty years.[25] And they were right. In 1233 the burghers of Rheims rose up against the excessive taxes levied by another church-building prelate; they forced him to halt the work for a time and to lay off the masons and image-carvers.[26]

However, the major role played by those hard-working peasants was fully recognized by all, particularly by the builders and stone-carvers. An image of the oxen used in ploughing, carved in stone, crowned the towers of Laon cathedral; and depictions of farmers' labour at different seasons appeared on the capitals of all cathedrals. It was only right to honour them in that way, for it was their labour that allowed the edifices to rise, little by little. 'Each workman, each farmer was a conqueror, and the cathedral itself meted out praise to him.'[27]

What about Louis VII, king of France from 1137 to 1180? Did he contribute significantly to the initial construction of Notre-Dame? Not so much, in fact. It was only with his son, Philip II (r. 1180–1223), whom Bishop de Sully baptised in 1165, that Paris became of real importance to the French monarchy. Louis VII was more interested in financing Cistercian monasteries than new cathedrals. And if Philip II too did not contribute much to the actual construction, the progress of which he could monitor from his royal palace on the Île de la Cité, he invested massively in the defence of his capital and his kingdom by erecting walls on the right and left banks of the Seine and fortresses such as the Louvre.

In fact, Philip II contributed greatly to the emergence of Notre-Dame cathedral, even before it was finished, as a symbol of power. In a very unusual move he chose it as the burial site of his wife, Isabella of Hainault, who died in childbirth on 12 May 1190.[28] Her grave was found on 19 February 1858 during the restoration works of Eugène Viollet-le-Duc. Buried alongside Isabella was her silver seal matrix.[29] That the king of France should choose to bury his wife in Paris's new cathedral with her seal matrix unbroken proved an exceptional event. Until then, no church competed with Saint-Denis-en-France for royal patronage. Since the time of Dagobert in the seventh century, Clovis's successors had chosen Saint-Denis as their burial place, and there the three dynasties which governed the kingdom of France in succession had continued to bury their dead. Charles Martel, Pepin the Short and Charles the Bald lay in the royal tomb near Dagobert and his sons, near Hugh Capet, close to his ancestors, the dukes of France, and his descendants, the kings.

However, Notre-Dame cathedral slowly started to rise in royal importance. Sons of kings began to be buried there, such as Henri II's son Geoffrey, duke of Brittany, and in 1218 Louis VIII's son Philip, count of Boulogne. And if Louis IX (r. 1226–70) put a temporary end to the ascendance of Notre-Dame in royal ceremonies, favouring Saint-Denis and Rheims, it was, however, deemed impossible to ignore Notre-Dame when his coffin was brought back from the Crusades in 1271 and paused in front of the cathedral. From the time of his coronation in 1285, Louis IX's grandson Philip IV (r. 1285–1314) chose Notre-Dame as a symbol of his royal and spiritual power.

*

'Anonymity suits cathedrals. No signature at the bottom of the façade, and no anniversary to celebrate. Builders carried out their professional duty and went on to build elsewhere,'[30] wrote the French writer Sylvain Tesson, who, in the early 1990s, as a young man fascinated by heights and summits, regularly used to climb up Notre-Dame at night.

We will never know the name of the architect who, under the direction of Bishop Maurice de Sully, drew up the plans for Notre-Dame. We will never know where he came from, whether he was the son of peasants like Sully or a relative of Louis VII, how he trained or the works he had accomplished before. All we can do is to appreciate the architect through his achievement at Notre-Dame. One thing is clear, though: Sully chose an architect who could understand and deliver his ambition for a new cathedral. We can easily imagine both men in intense discussions and meetings, which will have produced a multitude of documents, even if they have now disappeared:[31] scale models, sketches, plans, details and elevations. Once agreed, the final plans will have been made into documents handed to the workers in charge of the site, such as the master stonemason and his cohort of carvers, splitters and cutters. The efficient pace at which the first decades of building took place shows that the builders were no doubt following clear, detailed plans and instructions and that there were between 100 and at least 400 men working on it, six days a week.[32]

Precision was of the essence. Maurice de Sully, feeling confident he could finance it all and with the mind of an urban planner, launched a small topographical revolution in the heart of Paris. A new cathedral was just one central element of a very ambitious project. Having just renovated the ancient cathedral, the baptistery of which dated back to the fifth century,[33] Sully decided that a completely new cathedral was in fact needed. With the Gothic makeover of the cathedral of Saint-Denis and the new Sens cathedral, the old Romanesque tradition belonged to the past. Young architects had a new ambition: to free the interior space of churches thanks to new techniques and a rational use of cross-rib vaults. They also wanted to give them new and meaningful carved and stained-glass decoration. Sully could not leave Paris behind in what promised to be both an architectural and liturgical revolution. He had also heard that much smaller cities north of Paris such as Noyon, Senlis and Laon had followed Saint-Denis and Sens and were embarking on these pioneering endeavours. In fact, this new Gothic art, or as it was to be known 'the art of France', created an intense rivalry among enterprising prelates. They all wanted a Gothic cathedral.

The legend goes that Pope Alexander III laid the foundation stone of Notre-Dame cathedral in April 1163 during a visit to Paris; however, the story is attributed to the fourteenth-century chronicler Jean de Saint-Victor, in other words writing 200 years after the event. Maurice de Sully, elected bishop on 12 October 1160, most probably didn't wait so long to launch his dream project. The construction is likely to have begun in spring 1161.[34]

In fact, the whole eastern part of the Île de la Cité became a huge building site. Sully's idea was to rationalize and reorganize the life of the diocese and its administration with a new, clear topography which was to remain in place for 600 years, until the French Revolution.

As Sully was adamant that the cathedral should remain open for religious services throughout the works, builders needed to dismantle the existing ancient cathedral while building the new one little by little, in sync. One of the many challenges was that the new cathedral, with its 5,500 square metres' surface area, was much larger than the old one. On the east front, things looked relatively easy. The diocese owned the land at the eastern tip of the island and it was just a question of demolishing what was there and starting to build. Work on the cathedral thus began right here with the elevation of the chevet or apse, which was finished when Robert de Thorigny, the abbot of Mont-Saint-Michel, visited in 1177. The monk, awestruck, wrote: 'If this monument is one day finished, no other will ever compare.' Five years later, on 19 May 1182, the pope's legate, Henri de Château-Marcay, and Sully consecrated the high altar. The eastern part of the cathedral was therefore completed, with its vaults, stained-glass windows and decoration carved in stone.

On the west front, however, the outlook was decidedly messier. Many houses had to be bought by Sully in order to be razed. Some owners weren't easy to deal with. Negotiations could drag on for years. Records show that one couple in particular proved difficult. Henri Lionel and his wife Pétronille agreed to exchange a number of houses they owned for another two, plus a piece of land in a different area of Paris. However, it took thirty years to finalize the deal as they regularly asked for more money and compensation; every time, the diocese relented.[35]

Sully also wanted to shift the axis of the new cathedral slightly to the north and, much more drastically, to move the new façade of the building 40 metres to the east, in order to create a large parvis in front – where the ancient cathedral used to stand. He had conceived the parvis as a space which linked the profane and sacred worlds. He had also planned to create the largest thoroughfare Paris had ever known, 6 metres wide, on an east–west axis, right opposite the future central portal of the cathedral. The idea was for pilgrims to see their church from far away and be drawn to it as to a magnet. The street would be called rue Neuve. Even Baron Haussmann, the despoiler of medieval Paris, was not able to completely erase the memory of rue Neuve from the Île de la Cité when he redesigned it in the 1870s. To this day, golden marks on the parvis's cobblestones show where rue Neuve used to run.

Sully's plans meant that he needed to be active on many fronts at once. Many battles had to be fought and many tasks carried out at the same time, the first being to tear down the old episcopal palace and build a new one on the south flank of the new cathedral. The waterlogged terrain meant that masons had to dig 9 metres deep in order to create a stable foundation. Work started there in 1164, and the new Domus Nova Episcopi was built in a few years.[36] Sully had also ordered the destruction of the seventh-century Hôtel-Dieu (a general hospital and hospice for the destitute) and the rebuilding of a much larger version, for which many more private houses had to be purchased for demolition. It was to be erected on the south side of the future parvis. With its own cloister and bakery as well as dormitories, refectory, infirmary and a few chapels, this Hôtel-Dieu was going to be the biggest of its time.[37]

Considering the intense pace of construction in the first four decades, it is widely agreed that there was probably no shortage of excellent skilled artisans; Parisian stonemasons were renowned in northern France for their talents. In addition, raw materials like logs for the beams were easy to find: the bishop and canons owned many woods and forests. The only costs came from the drying of timber and its transportation. As for stone, Paris was surrounded by quarries of fine-quality limestone which was easy to transport by boat on the river; a small temporary port was even built at the tip of the Île de la Cité for this purpose.[38]

*

The original designs drawn up around 1160 for Notre-Dame must have commanded immense respect as they were then followed through, without any fundamental structural changes, by the three consecutive architects who carried out her century-long construction. Today's façade, from the portals up to the upper gallery and twin towers, still belongs to its design architect. Only the sculpted decoration isn't true to the original designs and was conceived in the early thirteenth century, at a time when a new concept of imagery emerged.

So who was this mysterious design architect? His oeuvre gives at least a clue to the characteristics of his personality: 'ambition, technical sophistication, clarity and serenity',[39] assesses the medieval historian Alain Erlande-Brandenburg. For, even if the initial momentum came from Bishop Maurice de Sully, the original architect was clearly eager and audacious enough to create the highest building ever erected in a city: 40 metres wide, 123 metres long and 33 metres high, with two towers reaching 69 metres. His skills allowed him to address technical challenges such as the boggy and unstable terrain of the Île de la Cité. A master of Gothic technique, he dramatically reduced the number of fulcra, or supports, within the cathedral. 'Never before had architecture managed to ensure the triumph of empty spaces over full ones.'[40]

The second half of the twelfth century was a stimulating time for architects and cathedral-builders in the north of France. The apse of Saint-Denis cathedral, under the direction of the dynamic Abbot Suger, had just been completed, setting a very high standard. The town of Laon in north-eastern France was also building its own cathedral, with ornate decoration. The creator of Notre-Dame de Paris had opted against such elaborate effects. He wanted to clear the interior space as much as possible, to declutter the cathedral, as it were. For the double ambulatory he had chosen very elegant tambour columns. Peacefulness emanated from this new verticality – verticality and harmony of proportion. The beauty of the nave is the result of a correspondence in architectural masses, their tiering, their receding and of course the superbly executed curves. 'Imagine the light of Île-de-France gliding on those naked white walls, playing on thin buttresses. Imagine the shock for those who, around 1180, going down the Seine River on their boat, suddenly faced this proud and powerful mass standing out against the ever-changing sky of Paris.'[41]

Still under the strict but dynamic tutelage of Bishop Maurice de Sully, a second architect took up the baton around 1177, supervising the erection of the eastern walls of the transept as per their creator's plans. He particularly showed a talent for details, as still seen today on the side piers with their elaborate decoration of carved leaves. His knowledge of stone and its properties greatly helped in strengthening and thus reducing further the size of the supports. For the transept's western pillars he chose *cliquart*, a Parisian limestone noted for its great resistance to weight and humidity; for the central nave's columns he selected rocks from Bagneux, the finest, whitest and hardest stone in Île-de-France. This second architect, as great as his predecessor, was succeeded by a third in around 1200, after the death of Sully.

The building of the nave was interrupted in order to concentrate on the construction of the façade. The third architect started building first the future façade's different supports: buttresses, pillars and the bearing walls which he then attached to the nave. He had achieved the first level, up to the kings-of-Judah gallery above the three portals, when he was replaced by a fourth architect in about 1210–20. The western rose window, many aspects of the two towers and the open-work spiral staircases in limestone bore the fourth architect's mark.

The names of the thirteenth-century architects who completed the cathedral *are* known: Jean de Chelles and Pierre de Montreuil erected the north and south façades of the transepts with their rose windows. In fact, each of Notre-Dame's architects tried to create a homogeneous ensemble, not simply to address one problem or mend one piece here and there. Each did it so carefully that it is sometimes difficult to discern who was responsible for what.

*

Now let's step back for a moment and look at the cathedral itself. Notre-Dame was different from all the other Gothic cathedrals that began to be built in twelfth- and thirteenth-century France. Although embracing the Gothic principles of light, space and clarity, Notre-Dame rejected the lavish munificence of Saint-Denis. Her serenity was almost austere. Her radiance didn't lie in the opulence of precious sparkling gems of the kind favoured by Abbot Suger but rather in the symphonic quality of her space. A special harmony and coherence would have struck anyone standing inside or outside. Perhaps because by the end of the twelfth century the art of cathedral-building had become also the art of the logician.

Cathedral architects showed that they were capable of applying theoretical formulas and of conceiving an entire edifice in the abstract. In fact, the 'doctors of the science of building', as they called themselves, had mastered the science of numbers that was taught in episcopal schools and universities. 'Each of the buildings they were responsible for erecting was a demonstration of Catholic theology, a transcription into inert matter of the professors' philosophy and dialectical thought process.'[42]

Yet for all their dexterity and virtuosity, architects and masons were following the vision of a circle of enlightened prelates such as Maurice de Sully. Notre-Dame cathedral was therefore a triumph of both logic and mysticism. Problems of statics and dynamics preoccupied them as much as those of elucidating the divine mysteries. In fact, both builders and clerics were inspired by both grace and truth.

Notre-Dame impresses itself on the viewer and the visitor through this marriage of minds, the secular and the sacred, but also through the union of solemnity and serenity in its ornamentation and austerity and majesty in its lines.

*

Now let's focus on a few details in close-up, for example the façade. On the right side, the portal dedicated to the Virgin donated by Abbot Suger of Saint-Denis was soon renamed Sainte-Anne. The Virgin's mother was indeed having a moment: in 1204 the Count of Blois had shipped from Constantinople a relic thought to be her head, and a cult of Saint Anne was fast developing in Europe.[43] Then there are the door fittings and hinges in cast and wrought iron, showing interlacing foliage, birds and small animals: masterpieces of elegance and lightness. The art of metalwork appears to have inspired many of Notre-Dame's image-carvers, especially with respect to drapery. It was all about creating volume and sharp edges in order to produce dramatic contrasts of light. The bodies of the saints, their movements, were in fact conveyed by the pleats and relief of their garments. For the figures of Saint Peter and Saint Paul in particular, the sculptor played with light by leaving bare spaces between two pleats in their robes. Sometimes the pleat was carved as sharp as a knife's edge, sometimes as round and soft as a rose petal.

On the left side of the façade, the portal of the Virgin showed for the first time in medieval iconography full head-to-toe statues of the most venerated saints in Paris, whose relics lay inside the cathedral. Indeed, Notre-Dame owned a whole collection of saintly bones – among others Saint Genevieve's upper arm and some of her phalanges, the top of Saint Denis's skull, the rocks with which Saint Stephen was stoned and hairs from the Virgin Mary's head, not forgetting a couple of Saint John the Baptist's teeth and a whole arm of Saint Andrew.[44] Interestingly, the stonework surrounding the doors is dedicated to earthly daily life with zodiacal signs and monthly farming activities, while on the central pier the different ages of life correspond to the four seasons.

The central portal, dedicated to the Last Judgment, higher and larger than the side portals, features the archangel Saint Michael weighing souls while Satan is seen openly cheating. The parable of the foolish and wise virgins adorns the door surrounds while depictions of vices and virtues cover the portal's base. In 1823, in his *Remarkable Details of Notre-Dame de Paris*, François Théodore de Jolimont wrote:

Hell is represented by an enormous dragon whose belly is a burning cauldron in which small devils, armed with forks, throw the Reproved, head down. However, what is even more remarkable in this bizarre depiction is the demon of Lust, characterized in such vigorous manner that it bewilders onlookers: are they really about to enter a place of worship? However, in those times of simple mores, those representations weren't more indecent than the pious usage the chastest of Roman ladies had of wearing gold phalluses around their necks.[45]

To see how the image-carvers of the twelfth century depicted Lust, you'll need to visit the cathedral herself, once she is reopened to the public.

While the cathedral of Saint-Denis overflowed with opulence, heaped as it was with royal donations, Paris's Notre-Dame rose from the ground thanks to a visionary bishop, his dedicated canons and the people. Notre-Dame therefore rightly 'embodied the townspeople's pride, as its plenitude of spires, gables and pinnacles thrust up toward the heavens a dream city, an idealization of the city of God which magnified the urban landscape'.[46] Its towers were a benevolent presence, guaranteeing the security of commerce within the city walls, and its nave was the only covered public space in the centre of town, for outside its house of worship each city was nothing but a tangle of narrow lanes, open sewers and pigsties.

*

The disastrous Hundred Years' War (1337–1453) would soon put an end to the greatest and longest period of continuous prosperity experienced in France. Notre-Dame would not be spared degradation. Some of her stained-glass windows would be torn down, her rood-screen, the choir enclosure and the stalls destroyed. However, Notre-Dame would be restored and rebuilt and, though she would come to be much pushed around and bullied by unkind souls through the centuries, Eugène Viollet-le-Duc would restore her to her magnificent medieval persona in the mid-nineteenth century.

3

1594 and 1638

The Bourbons

'Paris is well worth a Mass!'[1]

Les Caquets de l'accouchée

I n the last phase of the French Wars of Religion (1562–98), Paris had become a symbol, a kind of Holy Grail. Whoever conquered it would be deemed France's only legitimate ruler and put an end to decades of civil war. Since the assassination of King Henri III on 1 August 1589, the country had fallen into anarchy. Two powers were fighting each other. On one side was the Catholic League (the Ligue), which included both moderates and extremists and controlled the capital city; on the other, Henri IV, king of Navarre – and at least, in theory, of France – a Protestant prince backed both by his brethren but also by 'royal Catholics' who owned the very rich agricultural regions of Chartres and the Beauce, south of Paris. Their respective military powers, of equal measure, even occasionally reinforced by foreign troops, had managed only to cancel each other out. The outcome of the war was not going to be decided on the battlefield; it could only be settled politically and religiously. Paris thus became the epicentre of a psychological and propaganda battle. A campaign full of passion ensued, aimed at convincing the undecided but also at moving the hearts of adversaries.

The French had long considered Paris as Christendom's second capital city. It was therefore inconceivable, argued the *Ligueurs*, that a Protestant king should preside over the destiny of Paris, and thus over that of France. While Henri IV's partisans readily agreed that Paris was 'the eye, the glory and the honour not only of France but of the whole of Europe',[2] they also pointed out that the city's prestige was deeply linked to that of the monarchy. Refusing to open its gates to Henri was therefore a mistake: it belittled Paris's influence and stature. Then the Ligue made a strategic error. It convened the Estates General (États Généraux) in Paris on 26 January 1593, which immediately prompted Henri to reach out to moderates in both camps. Henri knew he had to act quickly, for the Ligue could very well decide to elect a Catholic king and crown him in Rheims. Henri asked the 'royal Catholics' backing him to enter negotiations with the moderate *Ligueurs* in Suresnes, to the west of Paris. As a result, Henri abjured Protestantism in July 1593.

The momentous news triggered a surge of support throughout the country and Catholic cities began rallying around Henri. With Paris still resisting, Henri chose the cathedral of Chartres for his coronation on 27 February 1594. The ecclesiastical anointing of the king strengthened his power further in the eyes of the people. However, Henri knew he still had to convince Parisians of his sincerity: he couldn't rule France without the support of Paris. He now had to plan his entrance into the capital.[3]

The principal *Ligueurs* having deserted Paris, the fruit was ripe for plucking. It was now only a question of gently taming those recalcitrant Parisians, but it had to be done in the right way. Just before dawn on 22 March 1594, Henri, accompanied by an army of a few thousand men, took advantage of a thick fog and light drizzle discreetly to approach two gates of Paris, Porte Neuve near the Tuileries and Porte Saint-Denis. The draw-bridges were lowered without much ado. Two detachments went in first to assess the situation in the capital, one marching down rue Saint-Honoré, the other along the riverbanks towards the Louvre. They had a few skirmishes with Spanish Catholic soldiers, but both units successfully joined up at Châtelet, on the Right Bank, opposite the Île de la Cité. The path was clear: Henri could now enter the capital on his horse.

Henri, unarmed but wearing a breastplate, calmly rode towards the Île de la Cité and allowed Parisians to approach him and his horse. People came so close that some could touch his stirrups. Shouts of '*Vive le roi!*' soon carried him, surrounded by an ever-growing crowd, towards the heart of Paris. He knew he had to go there first before settling into the Louvre. As he turned left into rue Neuve, the bells of Notre-Dame started chiming. The news of his arrival had reached the canons and archdeacon, who were ready to greet their king.

As he dismounted, did Henri recall the day of his marriage to Margaret of Valois twenty-two years before on 18 August 1572? He was standing right there, at the same spot, on the parvis of the cathedral where Cardinal de Bourbon, his uncle, had had to proceed to the royal wedding, for he was Protestant and she was Catholic. Margaret had then gone inside and attended Mass while Henri and his Huguenot entourage had stayed outside, waiting for the bride in the episcopal courtyard. Six days later, the Saint Bartholomew's Day Massacre against the Protestants, which occurred right in the heart of Paris and quickly spread to other cities in France, had shaken the country to the core. It also forever cursed Henri's marriage, which was later dissolved. Many French people had perished in the bloody wars of religion that followed that fateful day.

This time, however, on that March morning of 1594, Henri, followed by his men and a huge crowd, entered the cathedral. He walked to the choir and knelt in front of the altar to pray for national reconciliation. The hymns and music of the Te Deum began filling the nave while he was still kneeling, deep in prayer. Thousands of Parisians had joined their king in *grâce et pardon* (grace and forgiveness), and many more, alerted by the bells, were flocking to the Île de la Cité.

Obeying a carefully thought-out plan, while Henri was inside Notre-Dame his men were giving out *billets* to passers-by. Printed the day before in Saint-Denis, the leaflets explained Henri's benevolent intentions to Parisians. He would not seek revenge and would not punish the *Ligueurs*; he simply asked them to leave the capital. And for those who could not read, town criers, posted at every crossroads, also relayed the news, shouting '*Grâce et pardon*'. Envoys were sent to the *Ligueurs* still present in Paris, ordering them to leave at once. The whole operation had been well prepared. The people of Paris were conquered peacefully, finally reconciled with their king. And while the *Ligueurs* would for a little while still hold the cathedral cities of the north of France such as Rheims, Henri had chosen to associate his dynasty, the Bourbons, with Notre-Dame, which had opened its arms to the newly converted Catholic.

The king was thus back in Paris, in the Louvre, and Paris was again the centre of power. It would take another four years to pacify the country completely, but on 22 March 1594 Henri IV triumphed in a decisive battle. That day he won over the minds and hearts of the people of Paris, who now called him 'Henri le Grand' (Henry the Great). And from now on, to mark this historic day, every year for the next two centuries a religious procession would depart from Notre-Dame to the convent of the Grands-Augustins on the Left Bank for a High Mass. This celebration in honour of a great king ended during the Terror of 1793.

*

Henri IV's son Louis XIII would further strengthen the ties between Notre-Dame and the Bourbon monarchy and the country. He had been thinking about ways of doing so since the autumn 1630, after he had recovered from a severe bout of ill health. He had written various drafts of a document which he called his Vow. On 10 February 1638 he finally revealed his intention in an official declaration: 'I am giving myself and my kingdom, first to God, then to the empire of the very powerful lady; I dedicate myself and my kingdom to Their Majesty, trust them to their assistance, and attest the perpetuity of my vow by erecting a monument for the world and the future.' And he added:

We hereby declare that by taking the very saintly and very glorious Virgin as special protector of our Kingdom, we particularly dedicate to Her our person, our state, our crown and our subjects [. . .] We will rebuild the great altar of Notre-Dame of Paris, with an image of the Virgin holding her precious son taken down from the Cross; we will be represented at Their feet, showing ourselves offering Them our crown and our sceptre.[4]

Assumption Day, 15 August, was then chosen for a special procession from Notre-Dame which all authorities were requested to attend. Louis XIII's decision not only sparked an intense worship of the Virgin Mary in France; it also relegated to the shadows of history a well-known and thus far popular pilgrimage to Chartres cathedral in honour of the Virgin. A special event added a miraculous aura to Louis XIII's Vow. After twenty-three years of marriage, his wife Anne became pregnant for the first time – with a boy, the future Louis XIV, the Sun King.

The monument imagined by Louis XIII was fittingly realized by his son, who wished to associate himself with his father's Vow. The sculptors Nicolas and Guillaume Coustou were commissioned to create the Pietà and statue of Louis XIII offering his crown to both Virgin and Christ, while Antoine Coysevox worked on another statue featuring Louis XIV on one knee. Both monarchs were placed on each side of the Pietà. The ensemble was particularly striking:

The Virgin Mary, right in the middle, has her arms stretched and her face turned towards the sky; the pain of a mother and her perfect submission to God's will are expressed in the truest and most sublime ways; she holds on her knees the head of her son and part of his body taken down from the cross; the rest of Christ's body is lying on a shroud: an angel on its knees, in the shape of an adolescent, with his wings partly opened, holds the Saviour's hand, while another painfully holds the crown of thorns [. . .] This marble ensemble is of particular elegance [. . .] and to the beauty of the shapes and contours the artists have added sublime grace and expression.[5]

The Bourbons would lavish all kinds of works of art and gifts on Notre-Dame. Paintings started covering every chapel, every pillar even, while the standards and banners of enemies, captured on the battlefield, were exhibited hanging low from the upper galleries above the nave. The fifteenth-century tradition of the 'Mays' was reprised in 1630. Every year the goldsmiths' corporation of Paris commissioned the most promising artist of the time to make a huge, monumental painting (4 × 3 metres) for Notre-Dame, and offered it during a ceremony on 1 May. The 'May' of the year would be placed next to the Virgin Mary. The tradition lasted until 1707 and the resulting seventy-six 'Mays' had to be despatched to different museums in France for lack of space inside the cathedral. Notre-Dame was therefore France's first unofficial museum, the first place where the people could admire art for free.

From then on, Notre-Dame outshone the cathedrals of both Saint-Denis and Rheims in royal ceremonial. Our Lady became the high place of national events, where the political more often than not overshadowed the religious in ambiguous proceedings which almost always benefited the power already in situ.

4

1789

Reason, Supreme Being and Wine

'The ceremony should have been religious, but it was almost all military.'

The storming of the Bastille on 14 July 1789 is an event engraved on French DNA and the world's imagination. But what about the day after, 15 July? Who remembers today that the people of Paris, who had just stormed the old prison, freed its prisoners and killed its guards, flocked to Notre-Dame and celebrated with a triumphal Te Deum? Led by their newly appointed mayor and president of France's first National Assembly, the astronomer Jean Sylvain Bailly, Parisians gave thanks to Our Lady for the revolution and the beginning of the end of the *ancien régime*. In so doing, they – more than ever before, and perhaps somewhat paradoxically – appropriated the cathedral as the people's palace, both on earth and in heaven. They were in fact maintaining the monarchy's tradition of holding a Te Deum at times of national drama, while completely reinventing its symbolism. The cathedral seemed to offer a bridge between past and present, and a window into a bright, revolutionary future.

During the revolution, Notre-Dame held a great fascination for the French imagination. Revolutionaries of all leanings did everything they could to partake of her aura. Which is probably the reason why, as extraordinary as it may sound, the cathedral seems never to have closed during the revolutionary period.[1]

In the last decades of the *ancien régime*, Notre-Dame had in fact become a symbol of the revolutionary debate, for it was the only place in Paris where the king would occasionally deign to appear before his people. Parisians had increasingly come to resent his absence from the capital. In medieval times and under the Valois dynasty (1328–1589) the people had been used to having both temporal and spiritual powers, king and clergy, close to them in the Île de la Cité and nearby on the Right Bank, at the Louvre; however, the last Bourbons had neglected Paris and its people, choosing Versailles instead.

Louis XIV had established both his court and the government in Versailles in 1682. The idea was to control both nobility and government and to dazzle visitors with Versailles's splendour. However, leaving the Louvre Palace was a strategic mistake for which his great-great-great-grandson, Louis XVI, would pay dearly a century later. Oblivious to the resentment his actions caused, Louis XVI hardly set foot in Paris. When he did, it was usually to go to special Masses at Notre-Dame with his personal escort of 100 Swiss Guards who kept so close to him, even in the choir, that nobody could see him. Another mistake. Then the monarch would leave immediately for Versailles, deserting Paris's royal palaces and his people.[2] This behaviour was increasingly perceived as condescending and contemptuous, and it fuelled the simmering discontent.

Less than a month after the storming of the Bastille, another momentous event shook France: on the night of 4 August 1789, in a few hours of pure elation, the National Assembly abolished feudal rights and the many privileges of the clergy and the aristocracy, brought personal servitude to an end and instituted equality of taxation. Towns, provinces, companies and cities also renounced their special privileges. And once again Paris turned to Notre-Dame to mark its importance. Only a few hours after this historic vote, a Te Deum was celebrated there to rejoice and give thanks. Revolutionaries were closely associating the cathedral with their achievements in a highly political manner, reclaiming for their cause the transcendental nature of the place. In fact, the celebrations at Notre-Dame conferred on political events a legitimacy that their leaders craved, both for themselves and to display to the whole of France and the rest of Europe. Neighbouring monarchies, aghast at political developments in France, needed reassurance. Notre-Dame provided some relief in the shape of historical continuity.

The 1,200 deputies of the first National Assembly were heartened by what they had accomplished in such a short time, from the end of special privileges to the Universal Declaration of the Rights of Man and the vote for the first articles of France's new constitution on 26 August; but they were frustrated by the delaying tactics of the king and the most conservative members of the Assembly.

Many revolutionaries thought it essential to bring the king back to Paris in order to be closer to his people and to reality. This was achieved during the crucial days of 5 and 6 October 1789. At 7 a.m. on 5 October, thousands of Parisians, mostly women, gathered in front of the Hôtel de Ville. Their demands ranged from the ratification by the king of the new constitution's first articles and the availability of more bread, to the return of the royal family to Paris and the replacement of the royal Swiss Guard by the National Guard under the command of the Marquis de Lafayette and the compulsory wearing of the tricolour cockade.

Soon, followed by 20,000 members of the National Guard, the women marched to Versailles to talk directly to the king. Louis XVI, frightened, responded favourably to the crowd's demands except for one: his family's move to Paris. He replied that he needed time to think it over. He didn't think fast enough. At dawn, the impatient and angry crowd, who had spent the night merrily drinking, turned to coercion: they killed two Swiss Guards and entered the private apartments of Marie-Antoinette, who rushed in her nightgown to Louis XVI's bedchamber. That was it: an ashen-face Louis XVI agreed. The crowd and the National Guard proceeded to 'escort' the hastily dressed royal couple and their children to the Tuileries Palace, where it was decided they would now reside. They would never see Versailles again.

Where the sovereign went, the government followed. With Louis XVI in Paris, the National Assembly was also transferred to the capital. And where did the deputies choose to hold their first session? In Notre-Dame's episcopal palace, built by Maurice de Sully in the twelfth century. Did the place strangely inspire their next move, perhaps? A few days later, in the archbishop's very home, they decided to nationalize all Church property. In exchange, the state committed to give a salary to members of the clergy and to finance those hospices and hospitals which were the responsibility of the Church. And to make their decision palatable to the many poor clergymen who, early on, had sided with the revolution, it was agreed that priests would be paid an annual salary of no less than 1,200 livres, almost double what they received from the Church.

In truth, the state, impoverished by plummeting tax revenues, had severe cash-flow problems and needed to fill its coffers. Selling Church property – and selling it to the people – had become both a financial necessity and a potentially popular move. That the deputies chose to debate and vote on such an important measure at Notre-Dame's episcopal home showed a certain degree of impudence, but also their deep-rooted belief that Providence and divine justice were on their side – the people's side.

The following months witnessed the same impetus towards state intervention in all matters of life, and especially in religious affairs. Monastic orders such as the Benedictines and, in essence, all religious communities considered non-useful (that is, those not performing any rites and sacraments, or a service of education or health care) were dissolved by decree on 13 February 1790. Going further, the National Assembly decided to nationalize, as it were, the Church itself with the creation of the Civil Constitution of the Clergy on 12 July 1790. It was a simple and rather Cartesian attempt to reorganize the Catholic Church of France by creating a new administration and financial framework under the authority of the state. It reduced, for instance, the number of bishops from 135 to 83, each diocese corresponding to France's new territorial administrative make-up; bishops and priests were to be elected by their parishioners and the newly elected clergymen were made to swear an oath of allegiance to the constitution and the state; anyone who refused lost their position. Many bishops resisted and were therefore considered outlaws. Louis XVI opposed the law but signed it nonetheless, out of fear.

After the first Mass celebrated by constitutional priests at Notre-Dame on 16 January 1791, the cathedral's nave was turned into a huge polling station so that Parisians could elect new priests and replace all those who had refused to swear the constitutional oath. The whole process took six consecutive votes, each one preceded by a Mass, and on 17 March the Constitutional Bishop of Paris, Jean-Baptiste Gobel, could at last celebrate the ordination of his colleagues at Notre-Dame. A witness was struck by the tone of the celebration: 'The ceremony should have been religious, but it was almost all military. So many drums and a whole regiment of the National Guard in the procession, and so few actual prelates.'[3] In fact, this wasn't so surprising: the day before, the pope had broken all diplomatic relationship with revolutionary France. Pope Pius VI, who had remained silent since the beginning of the revolution, had finally condemned the Civil Constitution of the Clergy, deeming it heretic, schismatic and sacrilegious.

This, together with the resistance of many French bishops and priests to the Civil Constitution, not only created a religious schism, with the co-existence of a refractory clergy considered enemies of the people and a constitutional clergy, but deepened the National Assembly's suspicion of religion *per se*. As the revolution grew more and more radical, so did its attitude towards Catholicism and the practice thereof.

The summer of 1792 was a turning point. The arrest of Louis XVI, who had been caught trying to flee the country with his family, was immediately followed by the creation of the first revolutionary tribunal and the appearance of the guillotine on place du Carrousel (facing the spot where the Louvre Pyramid now stands). On 21 September the monarchy was abolished and the First Republic proclaimed. The trial and execution of the monarch were to be only a matter of months.

To counter attacks on her borders by her neighbours, almost all absolute monarchies vowing to crush the young republic, France's deputies ordered the mass call-up of 300,000 men on 24 February 1793. Within France, they were fighting on another front: that of the counter-revolution emanating from the Vendée region. Fighting both a civil war and conflicts with hostile, powerful neighbours, French deputies had little time for dissent and imposed the Terror in order to quell all opposition. The refractory clergy were among the enemies of the people, but so too were conspicuous religious and monarchical symbols.

The Terror didn't spare Notre-Dame. First, all its bells and bronze art objects, such as crucifixes and lecterns, were ordered to be melted down to make cannon, then all the lead coffins in the chapels suffered the same fate in order to make bullets. On 8 March, after France lost decisive battles in what is now Belgium, the cathedral's towers were partially wrapped with a black sheath as a sign of national mourning. The revolutionaries were slowly transforming the cathedral in their own image. On 23 October the beheading of the twenty-eight kings of Judah on the cathedral's façade, wrongly thought to be kings of France, was ordered by decree. They were duly decapitated one after the other by a stone-cutter. Soon afterwards the spire, dating back to the fifteenth century, was also demolished, but for a purely practical reason: it had become so frail that it could fall at any moment. Notre-Dame's appearance was definitely being altered. Behind the scenes, though, a few good souls were at work protecting the cathedral from more destruction.

Among the former priests of Notre-Dame who had sworn the constitutional oath out of convenience, many were intent on discreetly looking after Notre-Dame and seeing that she survived the revolutionary storm. While the organist constantly played revolutionary songs to please both officials and *sans-culottes*, others discreetly put away relics and statuary. The monumental marble ensemble, 'The Vow of Louis XIII', for instance, vanished from the choir; the 28-year-old self-taught archaeologist and medievalist Alexandre Lenoir had seen to that. He had convinced the first mayor of Paris, Jean Sylvain Bailly, and then the National Assembly that all confiscated art objects should be gathered in one place for safekeeping; he had suggested the former convent of the Petits Augustins. The revolutionaries liked the rationality and centralizing logic behind Lenoir's proposal and gave their approval. What they didn't know was that Lenoir took every opportunity he had to recover works of art from looters, or anticipate the pillagers' moves and put the objects in a safe place before they were either taken or destroyed. After the Terror had passed, in 1795 he finally opened the Museum of French Monuments, which was filled with all those treasures; it became France's second national museum after the Louvre.

On 7 November 1793, Jean-Baptiste-Joseph Gobel, bishop of Paris, was arrested in Notre-Dame's episcopal palace. This didn't bode well for religion in France, even the constitutional variety. Indeed, three days later Catholicism was abolished and forbidden. There would now be only one authorized faith in France: that of Reason. Whereas the churches of Paris were closed down, Notre-Dame remained open, immediately being consecrated to the new deity: it was now to be referred to as the Temple of Reason. The day after, French deputies voted to organize a ceremony to honour Reason, 'emancipated from slavery's prejudices and fanaticism'. The decree stipulated that 'the National Guard's musicians would come to sing patriotic songs in front of the statue of Liberty, raised at the same place where the statue of the Virgin Mary used to stand'.[4] The ceremony was scheduled for 12 November, or 22 Brumaire Year II. Reason-worshippers had two days to decorate both the nave and choir.

To witnesses, it was a decidedly 'strange celebration'.[5] A kind of mountain, or promontory, covered with grass was erected in the nave. At its top, a small Gothic temple had been built where busts of philosophers on pedestals were solemnly towering over the public. The words '*À la Philosophie*' (To Philosophy) had been carved on the temple's capital. On the side of the 'mountain' had been placed an enormous real rock, used as a base for a round altar on which a torch – the torch of truth – was burning. At a signal, teenage girls wearing white dresses and crowned with oak garlands, each holding a torch, started descending the mountain in pairs. Through the central doors, suddenly opened, a 'beautiful prostitute' symbolizing Reason entered and walked towards the choir, which had been transformed into a lawn. There she sat while music was played. At the end of the hymns sung in her honour, Reason walked up the mountain to the Gothic temple and turned back to smile at the crowd. Cue: end of ceremony. The words 'ridiculous', 'grotesque', 'inane', 'repulsive', 'horrible' and 'sacrilegious' sprang to the minds of many witnesses who related the event afterwards.[6] Secularizing religion was never going to be an easy task, even for French republicans.

Weeks and months of similarly curious celebrations and events followed. It was decided, for instance, that Notre-Dame would also be used as a lecture hall for conferences on morality by magistrates, and that legislators would read every law they passed to the public at Notre-Dame. Remarkable events would be specially celebrated, such as the abolition of slavery in February 1794. However, the worship of Reason was soon swept away by another 'faith': that of Robespierre and his Supreme Being.

As the Terror reached its climax, Notre-Dame was reconsecrated yet again in May 1794, this time to the worship of 'the Supreme Being and the Soul's Immortality'. Soon afterwards, while ceremonies in honour of the Supreme Being were performed, part of the cathedral was put to use as a warehouse for wine confiscated from émigrés, the many aristocrats who had fled the revolution: in 1794 and 1795, 1,500 barrels were reported to have been transported to Notre-Dame's side chapels,[7] which offered ideal conditions for storing wine.

Robespierre, finally falling victim to the monster he had created, was guillotined on place de la Concorde on 28 July 1794. The Terror fizzled out and a year later, on 15 August 1795, Notre-Dame was finally restored to Catholicism, albeit strictly controlled by the state. Napoleon quickly understood that national reconciliation regarding Catholicism was essential; in 1802 he would astutely strike a deal with Pope Pius VII. And, like all French leaders before and after him, he would use Notre-Dame as a magnificent stage.

5

1804

The Coronation of Napoleon

'Vivat imperator in aeternam!'

'We have reached the end of the revolution's narrative; we must now begin its history. We must implement its principles by being real and practical. We must govern, not philosophize.' This is how the 30-year-old Napoleon Bonaparte addressed France's state councillors the day after the 9 November 1799 coup, known as the coup of 18 Brumaire, under the new revolutionary calendar.

Now first consul of France after a bloodless and masterful coup d'état overthrew the Directory (the five-member committee that had ruled France from 1795), Napoleon Bonaparte officially proclaimed the new constitution of the French Consulate: 'Citizens, the revolution is fixed to the tenets which started it. It is therefore ended.' This new constitution, founded on the principles of representative government, equality, liberty and the right to private property, could only be guaranteed, in the eye of the new regime, by a stable government.

The young first consul knew that one of the most pressing issues he faced was the religious crisis that had been brewing for ten years. France, the most prominent Catholic country of the time, had to settle its relationship with the pope. It was in everybody's interest to do so. Napoleon also needed a political alliance with the Church, but one which acknowledged the disengagement between religion and monarchy. The French might still be attached to Catholicism, but they had overthrown the *ancien régime* once and for all. The Church had to accept this, and it also had to recognize the authority of the French state in matters of education and social order.

The election of a new pope in March 1800 was going to help. Pius VII wanted to restore the Church's unity, in which France necessarily played an essential role. The French Revolution had proved traumatic for the Church. First it lost all its properties, then, powerless to oppose, it witnessed the creation of a constitutional clergy whose members were appointed by the French authorities. The secularization of the state in 1794 meant that the practice of Catholicism was strictly confined to people's homes. What Pius VII prayed for was the end of what he saw as 'the French schism', and for Catholicism to be freely worshipped in all of France's churches.

After yet another military victory, this time at Marengo in Piedmont, on 14 June 1800, Napoleon sent the pope a conciliatory message. Negotiations with the pope's envoys started in earnest in November in Paris. For eight months, twenty-one different projects were examined and discussed. The issue of Church property was quickly resolved: the Church accepted its nationalization in exchange for usufruct and a state salary for the members of the clergy. However, the pope was adamant that Catholicism should be declared France's state religion, with its clergy appointed by Rome. Napoleon categorically refused, threatening to convert the whole country to Protestantism and to invade the Papal States. The impasse was total.

However, Napoleon knew it was time to give their religion back to the French, who missed its daily rituals and traditions. On 21 June 1801 a petition did the rounds in Paris which was signed by almost all the inhabitants of the Île de la Cité: they demanded that the bourdon Emmanuel ring again. Parisians missed hearing Notre-Dame's bells, and it didn't matter if they merely rang to announce public celebrations decided by the government, as long as the cathedral chimed again.[1]

More diplomats gathered around the negotiating table, mostly to work on the wording. The pope finally agreed that Catholicism would not be declared France's state religion, but only 'the religion of a majority of French citizens'. However, he wanted its practice to be public and free. Napoleon's brother Joseph found the words that would appease the first consul: 'Catholic worshipping must abide by police rules and not undermine public order.' At midnight on 15 July, an agreement, known as the Concordat, was signed by both parties.

A papal bull was immediately passed by the pope, but it took eight weeks for the first consul to ratify it and a further seven months for France's assemblies to pass the bill as law. The text, finally adopted on 8 April 1802 by French legislators (by 228 votes to 21), had, however, been heavily amended, with seventy-seven new articles. These had been added by some irreligious deputies. In short, they rendered the French church a national church, as impervious to Rome's authority as possible, and under the strict control of the civil powers. They stipulated that the pope was in no way infallible, that he must respect national traditions, that he could not depose heads of state nor ask Catholics to rebel against their country's laws and obligations. Gallicanism[2] had thus returned through the back door.

The pope felt extremely bitter, but the French were truly happy to rekindle the customs and traditions of their beloved religious celebrations. And Napoleon was intent on making a good show of it. A few days later, on Easter Sunday, 18 April 1802, the first consul, the whole legislative body, senators, judges and every Parisian authority attended a magnificent Mass of celebration at Notre-Dame, led by Cardinal-Legate Giovanni Battista Caprara. It had taken a few weeks to prepare and stage the event. The cathedral, 'in a lamentable state',[3] needed a lot of decoration to hide its decay and general dereliction. 'The nave was dressed with huge tapestries from the Gobelins manufactory, and paintings were brought from the Louvre.'[4] The throne of the first consul, flanked by four *fasces*, lay beneath a golden canopy; Napoleon sat opposite the cardinal. On a simple altar stood six silver crosses, each 3.6 metres high. Between the nave and the choir, Napoleon's family sat in an official rostrum erected for the occasion. 'The first consul's mother was placed so she could see all of her five sons, gathered here in solemnity. She seemed the intercessor between them and God, who had given them to her.'[5]

The cardinal-legate celebrated a Low Mass, and after the reading of the Gospel six archbishops and ten bishops were called one by one and stepped forward to swear an oath to First

Consul Bonaparte. The symbolism couldn't be clearer: if Napoleon had allowed Catholicism to return to the heart of France, it would, however, be under the command of civil authority, his command. As the last prelate bowed to Napoleon, two orchestras of 150 musicians, sitting on raised platforms on either side of the choir, started playing the Te Deum. The French and Italian composers Étienne Méhul and Luigi Cherubini, two leading lights of the time, each conducted an orchestra. As the Te Deum rose through the nave to celebrate the signing of the Concordat and the reinstatement of Catholic worship in France, Gilbert, the bell-ringer of Notre-Dame, was observing from the upper gallery. He recalled the event in his memoirs: 'France is at last reconciled with Europe and Europe with itself.'[6] As for Napoleon, as ever the pragmatist, he ordered two days later that his bathroom be transformed into a private chapel 'with a religious painting or tapestry to cover the mirror'.[7]

*

The two years that followed were filled with intrigue. Napoleon was set on invading England, and England on having the French leader assassinated. *L'armée d'expédition d'Angleterre*, as Napoleon referred to it in his correspondence with his generals, was getting bigger and bigger. At its height, the French flotilla comprised 1,831 crafts of all descriptions and 167,000 men. Camps for the invasion forces were set up in Boulogne and all of Normandy, and Napoleon inspected them regularly, checking everything, from the fortifications to the sanitary arrangements and the wine supplies. He loved talking to his men, mixing with them freely, and wanted them to be treated well. He had estimated that 'the invasion of Britain would require 300,000 pints of brandy'.[8]

All the leading French admirals opposed the English expedition. France may have had 'six centuries of insults to avenge', as Napoleon wrote in a letter in November 1803,[9] but all previous attempts had failed or been abandoned: Louis XIV in 1692, Louis XVI in 1779; even Napoleon himself had looked at the possibility in 1797. One hundred thousand or so Frenchmen would not be enough to conquer seventeen million Britons who had been preparing for such an invasion with garrisons in every southern town, fire beacons, stockpiles of provisions and defence breastworks dug around south London.

England was preparing in other ways too. By sending murderers to Paris. The assassination attempt was foiled in time. Napoleon was used to them and he could rely on his very efficient secret police, commanded by Joseph Fouché, to forestall such attacks. However, this one had particularly infuriated the first consul. The rumour that the Duke of Enghien, a direct descendant of Louis XIII and grandson of the Prince of Condé who had commanded the émigré army at the Battle of Valmy, might be involved in the plot stung him to the core. It was time to show the Bourbons that Napoleon's blood was the equal of theirs. The duke was swiftly abducted from Ettenheim in the Germanic region of Baden, where he lived, and brought to Vincennes, east of Paris. His seized papers showed that he was clearly living for the moment when Napoleon would be dead, that he was receiving a large amount of money from London and that he had offered to serve in the English and Austrian army against France, but there was no sign of his involvement in an assassination attempt against the first consul. Nonetheless, this was enough – ample evidence for a court martial to try him for treason; the duke confessed and was executed in the night. For many close observers the duke's death was a tragic mistake, as liberals across Europe would as a result start perceiving Napoleon differently. 'It was worse than a crime; it was a blunder,' said Fouché.

French senators were beginning to think that 'another institution' might be needed to destroy the hope of any future plotters; in other words, they deemed a kind of hereditary rule necessary to secure the revolution's legacy and guarantee the stability of the state. A state-sponsored campaign started preparing public opinion for a change of regime. But of what kind? A monarchy with Napoleon as king was out of the question. The Conseil d'État settled on an empire and an emperor, nothing less. An end should be put to the hopes of the Bourbons, explained Napoleon to his republican generals. As for the French who might object, they were promised the opportunity to vote against it in a plebiscite.[10]

On 18 May 1804, eight days after William Pitt the Younger returned to the British premiership committed to building a third coalition against France with the help of Russia and Austria, Napoleon was officially proclaimed emperor of the French 'through the grace of God and the constitution of the republic'. The ceremony, at Saint-Cloud, took fifteen minutes. Napoleon appointed fourteen marshals of the empire representing different political families, Jacobin and republican. Apart from two aristocrats, many were of working-class origins, sons of coopers, peasants, tanners, brewers, inn-keepers and servants, showing the meritocratic nature of Napoleon's empire. He addressed them all in his correspondence as '*mon cousin*'. Napoleon personified an exceptional symbiosis of French history, a reconciliation of normally opposed forces.

*

Now that he was reconciled with the pope, at least officially, Napoleon could ask him to officiate at his coronation and that of his empress, Josephine. When he wrote to Pius VII to invite him, Napoleon didn't specify the location; in fact he hadn't decided yet.

> Highly Holy Father, the happiness in which morality and my people's character find themselves after the reinstatement of Christianity on our shores prompts me to invite Your Holiness to express further interest in my destiny and that of this great nation, in one of the most important occasions the world will have seen. I am requesting Your Holiness to bestow religiousness upon the coronation of the first emperor of the French people. Your presence will enhance the ceremony's lustre, and draw upon our people and ourselves the many blessings of God, whose decrees dictate the fate of empires and families. Your Holiness knows the affectionate feelings I have long had for Him, and thus must understand the pleasure this opportunity will give me to express my affection further.[11]

The devil might be in the detail, but Napoleon had eagle eyes. When the grand master of ceremonies, Louis-Philippe de Ségur, confided to him that the whole ceremonial would have to follow the traditional coronation procedure called *Pro Rege Coronando*, by which the political supremacy of the pope is expressed in obvious ways (Napoleon kneeling before the pope and kissing his hand), Napoleon decided 'to adapt' this ceremonial 'to today's mores and traditions'[12] in a way that would not vex the pope too much. In fact, he intended to crown himself emperor. Even if the act of self-coronation was not unprecedented in Europe – it had been done before by Spanish kings and Russia's tsars – it had never been performed in the pope's presence. If anything, such a gesture would show the audience and the world that Napoleon owed his power to his military victories, his political achievements and his destiny alone. Besides, his coronation would be glorified by popular plebiscite, and to underline this Napoleon intended to crown himself not in front of the pope and the altar, therefore before God, but instead with his back to the pope, facing the public. After he had crowned himself and then Josephine, Napoleon's closest marshals would hand him Charlemagne's regalia: his crown, sceptre, sword, talisman and imperial globe. Napoleon clearly saw himself as a direct heir of the Roman and medieval emperors, never mind the Capetians – after all, their lineage had died with Louis XVI.

In truth, there was little left of Charlemagne's regalia. The revolution had seen to it. When Napoleon's envoys arrived at Saint-Denis cathedral and opened the treasury where the cache should have been, it was empty. They eventually found some bits and pieces in the museum: spurs, a sword and part of the sceptre were intact, but the crowns and Hand of Justice had been destroyed. Not a problem, replied Napoleon's jeweller, Martin-Guillaume Biennais. He found old prints of them and created new ones, except that he told everyone he had merely 'restored' them to their former magnificence.[13] He worked hard, though, and managed to find forty medieval cameos for Charlemagne's (new) crown.

Where should Napoleon hold what he envisaged as the most majestic of ceremonies? He had a formidable idea: what about Aix-la-Chapelle? After all, he saw himself as the restorer of the Western Roman Empire. His constant concern was that of the legitimization of his power. The ceremony would need to be a communion between the people and their emperor through a highly symbolic event. What he always tried to achieve was a synthesis between republican and monarchical pomp. However, the pope's refusal to set foot in the Lutheran Rhine region put an end to this mad dream.

Napoleon would crown himself in Paris, at Notre-Dame cathedral. This would satisfy both Catholic and revolutionary France. As for Rheims, it had definitely lost its place in the French pantheon, being too much associated with the memory of the *ancien régime*.

Work on decorating the cathedral began three months before the ceremony, under the supervision of Napoleon's personal architects Charles Percier and Pierre Fontaine, creators of the neo-Classical *style Empire*. The painter Jean-Baptiste Isabey, tutor to Josephine's children, gave them a hand. On 24 August it was decided that the interior looked too dark and that white-washing of the walls and vaults, previously done in 1780 and 1728, should begin at once. Each consecutive whitewashing unfortunately ate away not only the medieval colours under-neath but also the frescoes.[14]

After the Concordat, Napoleon had ordered that sculptures and paintings which had been removed during the revolution should be returned to the cathedral. The marble-mason François-Joseph Scellier had been commissioned to create a brand-new altar styled by the neo-Classical architect Etienne-François Legrand, adorned with bas-reliefs in gilded copper. As for the monumental marble ensemble 'The Vow of Louis XIII', it had made a very symbolic comeback in the choir. Still, there remained much to be done inside and outside the cathedral for the great event, which was now set for 2 December 1804. The invitation read: 'The divine providence and the empire's constitutions having bestowed the hereditary imperial dignity upon our family, we have fixed to the eleventh day of the month of Frimaire the ceremony of our coronation and crowning.'[15]

A year earlier, the Hôtel-Dieu across the parvis had been partly demolished and its façade rebuilt, but this renovation didn't go far enough. On 1 October, a few houses that were deemed to be standing too close to Notre-Dame's portals and obstructing the full view of the façade were knocked down. In front of the cathedral, a long porch, the full width of the façade, was erected. It formed three Gothic arches supported by four pillars. Adorning the pillars, thirty-six statues stood for the thirty-six towns whose representatives were invited to the ceremony. Statues of Charlemagne and Clovis I surmounted the two biggest central pillars and greeted visitors. Above each arch stood a pyramid on which rested Napoleon's imperial eagle. The imperial banner flew high on its tall pole placed between the two towers.

Inside, every inch of stone was covered with precious fabric – curtains, banners, hangings, veils, tapestries, canopies. The medieval marble floor was hidden under carpets, and even the 33-metre-high vaults were swathed in draperies whose gold fringes were spangled with the golden imperial bee, a Merovingian symbol which Napoleon gladly appropriated to replace the fleur-de-lis of the *ancien régime*. All around the nave ran three-tier grandstands, covered with rich gold-embroidered silk and velvet damask. At the nave's entrance, right at its centre, the imperial throne stood twenty-four steps high, beneath a triumphal arch supported by eight columns. The pope's throne was placed on a noticeably lower platform, eleven steps high, to the left of the altar. Five hundred musicians and choristers would take their seats on both sides of the transept crossing, while twenty-four chandeliers would illuminate the cathedral. On 24 November, to perfect this ephemeral and sumptuous decor, Napoleon made a gift to Notre-Dame of a pair of splendid gilded silver vases studded with diamonds. Bling was an imperial requisite.

And it included the guests' garments. Satin, silk and lace were *de rigueur* for the imperial couple, while astrakhan fur, ostrich plumes and precious gems covered dignitaries in a firework of colours: violet and green, blue and red contrasted with the whiteness of silk stockings and the blackness of felt and fur hats. Napoleon's personal architects and painter had designed everyone's attire.

For Josephine's satin dress Jean-Baptiste Isabey had found inspiration in Catherine de Medici's style, with a high collar, or *collerette*, framing the shoulders and neck; it had puffed-out upper sleeves embroidered with diamonds. In fact, she was covered with them: a thin comb in diamonds held her hair in a chignon while on each wrist she wore a diamond bracelet. Not to mention pendant earrings, a belt and, of course, her diadem made of 'diamond leaves'.[16] From 17 November, Parisians could go and admire all of Josephine's coronation jewels close up by pressing their faces to the window of Au Vase d'Or, the shop of her jeweller, Bernard-Armand Marguerite, which stood at 127 rue Saint-Honoré. He had put them on display with four fusiliers on guard, regulating the crowds, which queued until midnight every day.[17] Of all Josephine's coronation jewels, only the empress crown had been kept away from too close inspection. What did it look like? An inventory of 1811 gives us a detailed description: from a gold band encrusted with eighty-nine pearls, eight gold palm and myrtle leaves formed a crown surmounted at its middle by a gold globe topped with a cross. The gold leaves, each adorned with emeralds and amethysts, were separated from each other by three big pear-shaped pearls. A year later, the painter Jacques-Louis David asked to have it in his hands when he started work on his masterpiece, *Le Sacre* (*The Coronation*).

As for the emperor, he would be wearing gold-embroidered white velvet slippers and white silk stockings beneath a long white satin gown sewn with gold thread. Collar, sleeves, cuffs and hem were richly embroidered with green and gold oak- and palm-leaf patterns alongside golden stars, lightning and laurel crowns. The imperial mantle that went over his white robe proved as spectacular as it was heavy. It weighed 80 pounds,[18] and only the most special of men would be able to endure a three-hour coronation ceremony with it on his shoulders, not to mention the crown on his head. Made of crimson silk velvet, the mantle with its 5-metre-long train was embroidered with hundreds of solid-gold bees. Green oak, olive and laurel leaves appeared in embroidery patterns encircling the letter N. The lining and hems were made of ermine from Russia.[19]

*

On 25 November, Napoleon went to meet the pope in the Forest of Fontainebleau. They were then driven together to Paris in the imperial coach. The Flore Pavilion in the Tuileries had been specially prepared for Pius VII, with every room decorated identically to his pontifical apartments at Monte Cavallo in Rome. For three days and three nights before the event, six battalions of grenadiers and light infantrymen under the orders of General Géraud Duroc guarded the access to Notre-Dame and the Île de la Cité.

On 2 December, at 6 a.m., guests started arriving under a fine snowfall. For four hours, 12,000 French and foreign dignitaries of all ranks queued to hand their invitations to the ninety-two officials.[20] They included representatives from the legislative bodies, judges from the Court of Cassation, and members of government ministries, the war commissariat, the Institut de France, the National Guard, the Légion d'Honneur, the diplomatic corps and the army.

At nine o'clock sharp the pope set off for Notre-Dame. He was preceded by his nuncio, Cardinal Speroni, on a mule, as per papal tradition. Except Speroni was fuming: the mule he mounted was dark grey and not pristine white as he had requested. The spectacle was not lost on Parisians, who couldn't suppress their laughter at the sight: 'Here was this character dressed in a purple cassock travelling on an undistinguished mule, flanked by liveried servants holding the reins. Wasn't the contrast between his attire and the simplicity around him some sort of juggling trick?'[21]

After a long and more dignified cortège in the French capital the pope finally arrived at Notre-Dame, where he was greeted by Monsignor Jean-Baptiste de Belloy. He had ample time to change as Napoleon and Josephine hadn't left their private apartments yet. Although not required by protocol, Pius VII had nonetheless been warmly invited by Napoleon's household to wear his mitre 'in order to add sparkle to the ceremony'.[22] In full attire, the pope entered the cathedral by the central portal, accompanied by four canons carrying a canopy above him. All the French clergy were present to welcome him as a setting of 'Tu es Petrus' (You are Peter) was played by the two orchestras. Kneeling on his prayer stool, the pope now had to wait for the imperial couple. He knelt for ninety minutes.

Midday struck when Napoleon and Josephine reached Notre-Dame. After they had changed from their morning *petits costumes* into their *grands costumes*, the ceremony could at last begin. Everybody stood as the imperial couple appeared; they took position in front of their respective thrones. The solemn Votive Mass and religious procession now started. Pius VII then made Napoleon swear an oath to look after the house of God, to which he replied with just one word: '*Profiteor*' (I promise). Next, Napoleon and Josephine both received from the pope's hands the triple unction: this was the solemn part of the coronation which very few people could fully view as it took place, on purpose, in a secluded part of the cathedral. Napoleon didn't want the audience to see him as a subject of the Church.

What followed was, in Napoleon's eyes, the real ceremony, in other words the political coronation. Walking up to the altar, he then turned his back to the pope to face the assembly, seized his crown and crowned himself. It was the ultimate triumph of the self-made man who owed his success to his talent alone.

After a moment he walked towards the kneeling Josephine and placed her crown on her head. As the hundreds of musicians started playing a march composed for the occasion by Jean-François Lesueur, and the bourdon Emmanuel rang louder and louder, the imperial couple walked up the twenty-four steps to their imperial thrones. The public, following their every move, looked up to their 'Jupiter', whose face and crown were spectacularly illuminated by judiciously placed chandeliers hanging from the vaults.

The pope then ascended the imperial throne, kissed the emperor and intoned: '*Vivat imperator in aeternam!*' (Long live the emperor!) There followed Holy Communion, which neither emperor nor empress took. The symbolism wasn't lost on anyone, especially as the pope and all the cardinals were now swiftly ushered into the sacristy, where they wouldn't be able to hear Napoleon pronounce his coronation oath and allegiance to the secular constitution and fundamental laws of the empire, including the Concordat which placed the state above the Church.

Notre-Dame had been chosen precisely for this reason: its vastness, with its double-ambulatory nave, upper galleries, chapels and sacristy, allowed a clever political use of space. As the astute *metteur-en-scène* (scene-setter or director) he was, Napoleon had thought of every detail, and people saw and heard of the ceremony only what they were supposed to, according to their rank. Notre-Dame became the symbol and site of the synthesis between civilian and religious power, a revolving stage in France's complex and multi-faceted political drama.

It was past three o'clock in the afternoon when the twenty-five carriages of the imperial cortège set off towards the Tuileries, followed by the ten papal coaches, this time without the mule. Despite the cold, the fog and the snow, Parisians were out en masse. Half a million of them thronged the streets to acclaim the imperial couple and admire their glittering coach, which was drawn by eight white horses with white plumes and red leather harnesses. The cortège frequently had to stop because of the dense crowds.[23] Two hours later, when Napoleon and Josephine finally entered their private apartments at the Tuileries, the emperor could at long last take off the 80-pound mantle that had almost crushed him to death, never to wear it again.

That day Napoleon, the victorious general and pacifier, the head of a modern state, the political genius, had achieved the feat of assuaging antipathies and putting an end to division and hatred in the national conscience. Who else but someone educated in royal schools and elected by a republican people could have accomplished such a finely balanced equilibrium?

On 7 December, five days after the coronation and by order of the interior minister, Notre-Dame's canon, Monsignor d'Astros, received a mysterious package, a token of appreciation from the new emperor. Inside were the crown of thorns, a piece of the cross, a small phial containing the blood of Christ, Saint Louis's scourge, his tunic and many other holy relics. The treasures, which had been kept since 1248 at Sainte-Chapelle, specifically built for this purpose by Saint Louis, were moving house for good. Napoleon was expressing his gratitude to the cathedral that had made him emperor.

*

On 22 February 1800, a student of the painter Jacques-Louis David had thrown himself from the façade of Notre-Dame's upper gallery with a note in his pocket saying that he had always wanted to die that way.[24] Did Napoleon's official painter or *premier peintre*, as was his title, think of his former student when he was asked to create the painting of his life? It in fact comprised four canvases that Napoleon had commissioned from the 56-year-old David two months before the coronation. The project was to keep David busy for four years.

Having requested and obtained a special box in the cathedral on the day of the coronation, David made dozens and dozens of sketches, drew group studies and took notes. He had also visited the cathedral a few days before the event to sketch the different *décors*. He then spent the year 1805 preparing his work. He asked an architect to help him with spatial composition, began painting separate portraits, looked for a new studio in Paris vast enough to house those four enormous canvases, and received his first advance of 25,000 francs to meet the costs. He took advantage of the pope's presence in Paris until April 1805 to ask him to sit for him, and in September moved into his new studio, for which he soon requested two big stoves. David's studio stood in the former chapel of the Collège de Cluny opposite the Sorbonne. He usually didn't paint alone; a cohort of his best students would assist him or visit and give their opinion. He had hired one of them, the young, talented and obedient Georges Rouget, who worked alongside him. On 21 December 1805, David finally began painting *The Coronation*.

As the history painter he was, David enjoyed doing research. Precedents for such ceremonies were scarce, so he went back as far as the Middle Ages and fifteenth-century illuminated manuscripts to find sources of inspiration to represent, among others, groups of prelates. With their traditional and timeless attire, they would provide the necessary link between the antique-looking emperor with his ermine-lined mantle and the members of the court, dressed in a faux-Gothic fantasy. Rubens's *Coronation of Marie de Medici in Saint-Denis on 13 May 1610* was another obvious source of inspiration.

David soon asked for a small-scale model of Notre-Dame's choir to be built in his studio. Inside, he staged little dolls to represent some of the 191 recognizable characters he would paint on the canvas, carefully studying the effects of light on their clothes and faces. In this, reconstituting the scene in relief, he emulated his hero, Nicolas Poussin. Apart from the emperor, the empress and the pope, more than a hundred dignitaries present at the coronation came to sit for David in his studio. He often required them to come dressed as they were on coronation day; he also requested Napoleon's crown and the imperial mantle to be brought for a day or two so that he could paint their every detail.

The central issue David faced was the attitude bestowed on the emperor in the painting: should he be shown crowning himself, or crowning Josephine? He in fact painted both versions. After long consideration and a discussion with his student François Gérard in summer 1806, the artist eventually chose the gentler and more chivalrous option. His assistant, Georges Rouget, scratched out the surface of the emperor's figure and David repainted the more gallant attitude. Giving so much prominence to Josephine over the emperor proved a political challenge; however, when Napoleon gave his official approval on 4 January 1808 the debate became merely an academic one and David could breathe a sigh of relief.

That day, 4 January 1808, Napoleon, having just returned from Venice, crossed the Seine to go and see the finished painting in David's studio. Accompanied by Josephine and a small entourage, the emperor is said to have exclaimed: 'One walks in this picture!' Imperial praise would definitely calm the critics. The last to leave the studio, after more than an hour studying the canvas, Napoleon turned to David and removed his hat to salute the artist.

What Napoleon had particularly enjoyed in David's work was both the attention to detail, and therefore historical truth, and the reinvention of the event with the presence of characters in the painting who had been so visibly absent in Notre-Dame. For a start, Napoleon's mother Letizia, who was in Rome at the time in protest against Josephine, whom she deeply disliked, was overlooking the scene of the coronation from a central box, smiling kindly at her son. This was how the event should now be recorded for posterity.

The Coronation was displayed first in the Louvre from 7 February to 21 March 1808 but then hidden from view until 1838, when it was finally given space at Versailles. In 1889 it moved to the Louvre, where it still hangs. Measuring 6.2 metres by 9.8 metres, it is the second largest painting in the museum, after Veronese's *The Wedding at Cana*.

*

Times were changing fast. On 2 September 1815, by order of King Louis XVIII, restored to the throne of France by Napoleon's enemies, a Solemn Mass was held at Notre-Dame to repent for all the outrages perpetrated against God during the revolution. A few weeks later, on 17 October, another Solemn Mass was celebrated, this time for the anniversary of Marie-Antoinette's death, to get the message firmly across to those rebellious Parisians. Louis XVIII's rule didn't see the return of the *ancien régime*, and he wasn't the absolute monarch his older brother, Louis XVI, had been. Still, for some the return of the Bourbons in France proved too much. On 18 April 1817, during the vespers at Notre-Dame, a poor *grognard*, a former soldier in Napoleon's Old Guard, cut his throat in the sacristy. The French would have to get used to the loss of their emperor.

6

1831

How Victor Hugo's Novel
Saved Notre-Dame

This Will Save That

The 32-year-old romantic painter Eugène Delacroix, a liberal and a Bonapartist, was only a witness, or a *promeneur* as he called himself, of the 'Three Glorious Days', also known as the July 1830 revolution. What he saw during those days, walking through the French capital, impressed him to the core: Parisians from all walks of life, artisans, workers, bourgeois, students, even children building barricades together, fighting to the death for freedoms King Charles X wanted to abolish. Louis XV's grandson, who had occupied the throne since the death of his more liberal brother Louis XVIII in 1824, wanted little by little to restore the *ancien régime*. He had started by restoring old Bourbon traditions, as shown by his coronation on 29 May 1825 at Rheims cathedral – pointedly not at Notre-Dame.

On 25 July 1830, the increasingly repressive monarch passed six highly contentious rulings: the first one re-established complete press censorship; the second dissolved the predominantly liberal parliament which had just been elected; the third restricted further the right to vote to the richest French males, thus withdrawing voting rights from the *petite bourgeoisie*, who were suddenly deemed insufficiently important to have a voice; the fourth, fifth and sixth introduced fundamental constitutional changes favouring the ultra-royalist party in many public institutions. The people took it for what it was, a provocation and an affront. Blood would run in the streets of Paris.

For three 'glorious' days, 27, 28 and 29 July 1830, the people of Paris rose up in arms. First, the press refused to bow to censorship and announced that from now on they viewed the king's power as illegal, and that their duty was to disobey, by force if necessary. Gendarmes were sent to the newspapers' offices to arrest the journalists of *Le National, Le Temps, Le Globe* and *Le Journal du commerce*, but the printing workers and typographers fought back, triggering the insurrection. Former members of Napoleon's Old Guard, who had kept their weapons as souvenirs or perhaps for other purposes, joined the ranks of the rebels, who had so far fought the Royal Guard only with bricks and cobblestones.

While Charles X stayed in the safety of his castle at Saint-Cloud, it became clear that the riots were growing into a revolution, with cries of '*À bas les Bourbons! Vive la liberté!*' (Down with the Bourbons! Long live Liberty!) Every royal emblem was splashed with mud, if not destroyed, and royal white flags with their fleurs-de-lis were burnt. Parisians stormed the Hôtel de Ville and raised the tricolour; garrison after garrison defected to the revolution; and the students of the prestigious Saint-Cyr military academy rallied to the people on the barricades.

French republicans were unable to unite, the 72-year-old Marquis de Lafayette having refused to lead them; so a group of deputies discreetly made contact with Louis-Philippe, the cousin of Charles X, of the Orléans branch of the Bourbons, which was notoriously more liberal. While negotiations were under way, with Charles X and his direct heir abdicating and Louis-Philippe accepting both the title of *Lieutenant Général du Royaume* and the conditions imposed by parliamentarians, thousands of Parisians stormed Notre-Dame's episcopal palace in an anti-clerical fit of rage aimed at Charles X, known for his religious bigotry. A few men hoisted tricolours at the top of the towers while many others went on the rampage, ransacking the archbishop's coffers, pillaging the silver and shredding the priests' ceremonial garments. The cathedral herself and the saintly relics were left untouched: a sign of respect from even the most rebellious and anti-clerical of Parisians?

At first Delacroix had felt fascination, but also much dread. However, as Alexandre Dumas revealed later, 'when Delacroix saw the giant tricolour flag raised on each of Notre-Dame's towers, enthusiasm engulfed his fear. This was Napoleon's flag! He would glorify this people who, at first, scared him.'[1] Those three days filled the young painter with awe and elation, vivid feelings that he would depict on a huge canvas a few weeks later: *Liberty Leading the People*, the painting which would become the symbol of the French revolutionary spirit in action, was taking shape in his mind.

Near the Champs-Élysées, at 9 rue Jean Goujon, the new home into which he had just moved with his wife Adèle, Delacroix's younger friend, the 28-year-old poet and playwright

Victor Hugo, was also thinking hard. On 25 July he had at last started work on a novel he had long promised his publisher, Charles Gosselin. He had five months to write it or he faced having to reimburse his publisher the advance, long ago spent, and also pay heavy penalties. His theatrical work, more closely connected to the tumultuous epoch he lived in and which was what really interested the fiery young Romantic writer, had totally consumed him until then. Now, though, it was time for him to embark on this new novel which, two years earlier, he had vaguely described as being along the lines of those of Walter Scott, wildly popular in France at the time.

He couldn't have chosen a more volatile time to set to work. Two days after he had written down the title, *Notre-Dame de Paris*, Parisians started building barricades, and soon Hugo's wife would give birth to their fifth child, who would bear her mother's lovely name, Adèle. As for Delacroix, the elation of those revolutionary summer days and the exciting political developments would fire up Hugo's inspiration and narrative powers.

He had chosen Notre-Dame not just as the setting for his story: the cathedral *was* the story and, along with the people of Paris, the heroine. As Hugo started building his storyline and characters – the beautiful, bohemian Esmeralda, secretly loved by the kind hunchback and bell-ringer Quasimodo, the vicious Archdeacon Frollo, the penniless poet Gringoire and the handsome but oblivious captain of the guard Phoebus – the author, too, seemed to be led by a higher motive and possessed by an otherworldly force.

It soon felt to Hugo as if the topic was outgrowing itself, as if he barely had control of the story, as if he couldn't stop the flow

The Right Hand of God Protecting the Faithful against the Demons (c. 1452–60) by Jean Fouquet (tempera and gold leaf on parchment). Notre-Dame can be seen in the background.

St Bartholomew's Day Massacre (c.1572–84) by François Dubois (oil on panel). The massacre of Protestants by Catholics in August 1572 took place only a few days after the Protestant and future Henri IV married his Catholic wife, Margaret of Valois.

Twenty-two years later, Henri IV entered Paris as King of France on 22 March 1594. The image shows him on his way to attend Mass at Notre-Dame (engraving by Jean Lecler, after Bollery).

The choir and the pietà in Notre-Dame (1723)
by the sculptor Nicolas Coustou.

Celebration of the Goddess of Reason at Notre-Dame cathedral on 10 November 1793, by Auguste Christian Fleischmann.

The Consecration of the Emperor Napoleon and the Coronation of the Empress Josephine on 2 December 1804 (1806–7) by Jacques-Louis David (detail from the central panel, oil on canvas).

Victor Hugo's bookplate, engraved by Ernest Aglaüs Bouvenne.

Project for restoration of the west façade of Notre-Dame cathedral (1843) by Eugène Emmanuel Viollet-le-Duc (pencil & water colour on paper).

Drawing for the restoration of the gargoyles of Notre Dame (1855) by Viollet-le-Duc (pen & ink on paper).

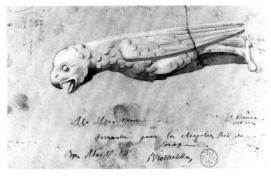

Restored gargoyles from the balustrade of the Grande Galerie of the west façade of Notre-Dame.

Notre-Dame on Turgot's Map of Paris 1739, showing the narrow streets in front of the cathedral.

The hospice of the Hôtel-Dieu before the clearances undertaken by Baron Haussmann and his successors (photograph by Charles Marville, 1874).

Photograph showing the newly created Parvis in front of Notre-Dame after the clearances (1894).

The Liberation of Paris – Charles de Gaulle arriving at Notre-Dame, 26 August 1944, moments before snipers try to assassinate him.

Gina Lollobrigida and Anthony Quinn in a scene from the film of *The Hunchback of Notre Dame* (1956).

The nave of Notre-Dame after the fire (2019).

of his thinking. This novel was going to be much more, and much longer, than he had originally planned. He asked Gosselin for more time and money for the extra length. His publisher, convinced it was yet another ploy to buy time, refused categorically. Hugo nonetheless continued to write and, after the release of Gosselin's edition in March 1831, immediately sought a new publisher to publish the full-length version. He struck a deal with Eugène Renduel, who was very keen to publish a richly illustrated edition featuring the work of the best artists of the time, such as the wood-engraver Henri Porret and the illustrator Célestin Nanteuil. He wanted the book, as an object, to mirror its literary content. The definitive edition of *Notre-Dame de Paris*, published in December 1832, with its richly adorned red cover, neo-Gothic vignettes and plates, was a cathedral of a book whose illustrations fired the imagination of the reader as much as Hugo's words did. People flocked to buy the affordable editions, with their powerful combinations of images and text. To open the Renduel edition was to enter a whole new world, intriguingly set in 1482.

Nothing of note had happened at Notre-Dame in 1482, nor for that matter in Paris. And yet Victor Hugo had chosen the fifteenth century and the reign of Louis XI to tell his story. Perhaps because it was a time when the cathedral was already suffering from 'the countless degradations and mutilations which time and men have simultaneously inflicted',[2] perhaps also because it was 'a transition period between the confusing end of the Middle Ages and the rude splendour of the Renaissance'[3] – a little like the mid-nineteenth century in France, trying to find a way to safeguard the legacy of 1789 in a modern world.

Hugo knew little about the Middle Ages, and it is fair to say that little was then known generally about the period. The famous École des Chartes, which trained archivists, historical scientists and palaeographers, had only been founded a few years earlier, in 1821, and scholarly knowledge about medieval times in particular was still lacking. Hugo brought home old history books about Paris by sixteenth- and seventeenth-century scholars such as Jacques du Breul and Henri Sauval, and the then well-known 'universal biographical dictionary' by Louis-Gabriel Michaud. He would build his cathedral with his imagination, peppered with real historical facts and real people, and then fill it with his own political and philosophical ideas.

Hugo proceeded joyously and expertly to weave together different literary genres. *Notre-Dame de Paris* was at once a Gothic novel *à l'anglaise*, a medieval chronicle, a love story, a treatise on alchemy, a philosophical essay and a political manifesto. The definitive edition of 1832 contained key new elements dear to Hugo, for example the famous Book Five and its chapter about how the printed word killed architecture, 'This Will Kill That'. In it, abandoning the narrative, Hugo addressed the reader directly. His thesis: from the beginning of history until the fifteenth century, architecture had been the book of mankind, from standing stones (representing letters of the alphabet), dolmens (syllables), groups of dolmens such as those at Carnac and Stonehenge (sentences), to whole buildings like the Egyptian pyramids, history's first 'books'. The invention of printing marked therefore the death of architecture, which had culminated in Gothic cathedrals, the last and greatest books of stones.

Strangely, and although the cathedral was the main heroine of his novel, Hugo only described the place in broad brush strokes, like a theatre set. He seemed in fact more interested in her mass, in her very idea, in her symbolism than in her details. Hugo did not take the reader by the hand for a special visit either. In fact, one had to wait until Book Three for an official introduction. 'On the face of this old queen of our cathedrals, beside each wrinkle you will find a scar,' Hugo wrote. For him, Notre-Dame was in fact a living being, half queen, half chimaera.

Victor Hugo wanted to achieve two things with his novel: first, to portray the Middle Ages in their authenticity, not in terms of the chintzy medieval fad that emerged in the early 1800s as a kind of cheap pastiche made of fairies, ruins and troubadours; and second, to raise awareness about the terrible state of historical monuments in France, left to crumble and then simply be demolished by property developers. They needed a thorough national plan of restoration and protection, and Hugo was to be their indomitable and selfless spokesperson.

He was particularly incensed by those supposed 'men of the art' who had mutilated the cathedral since the fifteenth century. 'But who cast down the two rows of statues? Who left the niches empty? Who cut that new and bastard ogive right in the middle of the central doorway? Who dared set within it that heavy, tasteless wooden door carved in Louis XV style, next to Biscornette's arabesques? The men, the architects, the artists of our own day.' In Book Three, Hugo drew up a long list of degradations inflicted by man. In fact, he distinguished three sorts of damage: 'first is time, which has chipped it away imperceptibly here and there and left rust all over its surface'. Secondly, the political and religious revolutions, which, 'blind and angry by their very nature, have hurled themselves upon it in tumult [. . .] smashed its rose windows, broken its necklaces of arabesques and figurines, torn down its statues, sometimes for wearing a mitre, sometimes a crown'. Thirdly, there had been silly and absurd fashions which did more harm even than revolutions:

> They have cut into the living flesh, attacked the bone structure of the art underneath, they have hewn, hacked, dislocated, killed the building, in its form and in its symbolism, in its logic as in its beauty. And then they remade it, a claim that at least neither time nor revolutions had advanced. Brazenly, in the name of 'good taste', they stuck over the wounds of Gothic architecture their wretched baubles of a day.

Hugo had nothing but contempt for those so-called defenders of 'good taste', those ignorant officials: 'The magnificent art produced by the early Vandals was killed by the academies [. . .] It is the ass kicking the dying lion. It is the old oak decaying, as a final blow being stung, bitten and gnawed by the caterpillars.'

With *Notre-Dame de Paris*, Victor Hugo was keeping up a fight he had started in 1825, aged only twenty-three. His pamphlet *Guerre aux démolisseurs!* (War on the Demolishers!), also published under the title *Sur la destruction des monuments en France* (On the Destruction of Monuments in France), had spelt out very clearly and passionately the urgency of saving old monuments in France. 'The time has come for everyone to stop remaining silent. A universal cry must now call for the new France to come and save the old one.' This fervent essay had been published many times since 1825, and was again in 1832 as a companion piece to *Notre-Dame de Paris*. It had a profound impact both on the new political regime of Louis-Philippe and also on public opinion.

Instead of erecting new edifices in the Graeco-Roman fashion, which at the end of the day are neither Greek nor Roman, why not save original medieval buildings that are uniquely French, argued Hugo. What he campaigned for was a new law that would prevent property speculators from demolishing historic buildings. 'There are two things in a building: its use and its beauty. Its use belongs to the owner, its beauty to everyone, to you, to me, to all of us. Therefore, to destroy it is to exceed one's rights.' In addition he called for auditing and supervision which could be performed as a public service by an institution or a specially dedicated department in a ministry, in short a monitoring unit.

Louis-Philippe, keen to found his political legitimacy on the double legacies of the 1789 revolution and Old France, saw in Hugo's campaign a way to achieve this. His prime minister, François Guizot, thought that only the state could lead such operations, with the help of local prefects and mayors. He therefore created the position of inspector of historic monuments, which the writer Prosper Mérimée (author of the novella *Carmen*) held from 1834, as we will see in the next chapter. It was time to save the Middle Ages and their truly original art from oblivion, time to show the French their extraordinary medieval legacy, about which they had forgotten.

Was it not to thirteenth-century Paris, and to the university around Notre-Dame, that the prelates of the Christian world, the bishops of Scandinavia, of Hungary, of Morea, of Saint John of Acre, of Nicosia, flocked in order to learn and gain enlightenment?[4] The papal prohibitions which had sought to ban from the university all Aristotle's treatises on subjects other than logic had been triumphantly defied, and Paris had become a magnet for independent-minded scholars and students. With its intellectuals claiming the right to philosophize, lay professors taught Aristotle's work to very young pupils, many of whom planned to pursue lay careers.

Finally, was it not precisely this university, right here on the Île de la Cité, which had shown a new, rational way to the idea of human happiness? Wasn't it from this university that thirteenth-century lay professors had proclaimed that thinking led to human dignity, freedom and goodness?[5]

Post-revolutionary and post-Napoleonic France could only welcome the opportunity to delve into such a strangely forgotten and yet glorious past, in which Notre-Dame held a special and symbolic place, for two main reasons. The first was because she offered both the beautiful and complex face of French history and also a synthesis:

Each face, each stone of the venerable monument is a page not only in the history of France, but also in the history of science and art. Thus [. . .] while the little Porte-Rouge goes almost to the limits of fifteenth-century Gothic delicacy, the nave pillars, by their volume and weightiness, go back to the Carolingian abbey of Saint-Germain-des-Prés. Anyone would think that there were six centuries between that door and those pillars. [. . .] This central, generative church is a kind of chimera among the old churches of Paris; it has the head of one, the limbs of another, the rear of a third; something of all of them.

The second was because Notre-Dame was the people's cathedral, making one feel that 'architecture's greatest productions are not so much the works of individuals as of societies; the fruit of whole peoples in labour rather than the inspiration of men of genius; the deposit left by a nation; the accumulation of centuries'.

Hugo's novel heralded the resurrection of medieval architecture, soon spearheaded by the young, self-taught architect Eugène Viollet-le-Duc. Hired in 1834 by the newly created Department of Historic Monuments, Viollet-le-Duc, a rebel against the academies, also belonged to those lovers of old stones who tirelessly campaigned to restore and treat medieval monuments with dignity. If Victor Hugo saved Notre-Dame with his book, Viollet-le-Duc would soon lead her restoration.

The success of *Notre-Dame de Paris* was manifold. Having achieved its aim of saving Paris's cathedral from certain death, it quickly grew into one of the first worldwide multimedia phenomena. The novel's characters and the cathedral started appearing everywhere: on plates, thermometers, ashtrays, figurines, clocks, posters, cheap prints and lithographs, among many other objects. A couple of months after its publication, Hugo reluctantly agreed to its adaptation for the opera. In fact, since 1832 it has been produced ten times on stage for theatre and ballet, a dozen times as a musical and another ten times on the big screen since the beginning of cinema – its most notable film versions being with Charles Laughton and Maureen O'Hara as Quasimodo and Esmeralda in 1939, and Anthony Quinn and Gina Lollobrigida in 1956. The 1996 Disney animation film *The Hunchback of Notre-Dame* guaranteed the passing of the torch to future generations, which may explain why Victor Hugo's novel has even provided hit soundtracks for Céline Dion and the setting for video games such as *Assassin's Creed Unity*.

The French often turn to literature in the wake of national catastrophes. After the *Charlie Hebdo* attacks in January 2015, sales of Voltaire's *Traité sur la tolérance* (Treatise on Tolerance, 1763), a pamphlet against religious fanaticism, sky-rocketed. After the 13 November 2015 attacks in Paris which left more than 130 people dead and 400 injured, Ernest Hemingway's *A Moveable Feast* topped the best-seller chart for months. The book's celebration of Paris, its insouciance and joy, spoke to millions of French people traumatized by the terrorist attacks. In the weeks that followed the fire of 15 April 2019, Victor Hugo's novel, reissued in a special edition with profits going towards the reconstruction, suddenly sold more in a couple of days than it used to in a whole year. This Will Save That: the book that keeps on looking after Notre-Dame.

7

1844

Viollet-le-Duc

'I wish my life would end right here in the rose window's light'

Eugène Viollet-le-Duc was born at 1 rue Chabanais in Paris, near the Palais Royal, on an icy afternoon in January 1814, a child of the enlightened bourgeoisie, Catholic by social convention more than by conviction, and mostly apolitical. On his father's side there had been civil servants and merchants; on his mother's, his uncle, Étienne Delécluze, had been a student of the painter Jacques-Louis David at the time of Napoleon's coronation and in 1822 had gone on to become the in-house art critic of the influential *Journal des débats*, a position he held for thirty-five years. A friend of the writers Stendhal and Prosper Mérimée, Étienne held a literary salon *d'esprit libéral* every Sunday afternoon at 2 p.m. in his attic above the Viollet-le-Ducs' flat.

Those young liberals, critical of the monarchies of Louis XVIII (1814–24) and Charles X (1824–30), were, however, more interested in the arts than in politics and, above all, curious about the world they lived in. Polymaths, they devoured literature and eagerly studied archaeology, botany and science. Mérimée, an accomplished pianist, had studied law but also Russian, English, Arabic and Greek, while his appetite for history, mysticism and the unusual was boundless. They didn't quite subscribe to Victor Hugo's style, which they deemed too emphatic; they advocated instead a kind of 'realistic romanticism'.

In his late twenties, Mérimée, already a successful short-story writer, decided to enter the civil service. This would enable him to write while earning a steady income, and to fulfil some lifelong ambitions. His passion for old stones made him the perfect candidate for the position of inspector of historic monuments. Created under France's new leader, King Louis-Philippe, in 1830, this new public service aimed to perform the long-needed task of assessing, listing and helping maintain France's vast number of historical monuments, some of which, like Notre-Dame, were in a terrible state of decay. Mérimée started his dream job on 27 May 1834, and swiftly toured the country in order to set up the first classification of the historic monuments and establish a budget for their preservation. This was the beginning of a long and glorious adventure.

The young Viollet-le-Duc wished to become an architect but didn't want to attend art school, namely the École des Beaux-Arts or the Académie de France in Rome, the two main artistic institutions which shaped French talent. He felt that those two schools, however prestigious, stifled individual creativity and imposed a particular way of looking at the world. Besides, the system of co-opting between professors meant that no original or dissenting voice could ever emerge. Eugène was a rebel.

Furthermore, his love for the art and architecture of the Middle Ages set him apart at a time when neo-Classicism was all the rage. The Middle Ages were seen as a *bizarrerie*, a world full of monsters, fear and irrationality, whereas he was convinced of the exact opposite. He had started studying medieval building and was full of admiration for what he saw instead as rationality and clarity.

Eugène wanted to break the mould, but how would he obtain an education in architecture? His uncle Étienne advised him to travel the country, observing, drawing, studying and painting, and return to Paris. And to show how this was done, over the summer of 1831 Étienne took his 17-year-old nephew on a three-month tour of discovery. They walked from the Auvergne to Provence, sketching every old church and monument en route. Eugène came back with thirty-five drawings. After his mother died of cholera the following year, the aspiring architect continued touring France; this time he chose Normandy and walked from Cherbourg to Le Havre and from Honfleur to Rouen. His drawings of landscapes, and also monuments, became better and better, and four of his drawings were exhibited at the Salon de Printemps in 1832. He had found his calling on France's small country roads. In 1833 he completed another three-month tour of the Loire valley, the Languedoc and the Pyrenees, bringing back 173 drawings.

Back in Paris, he took up a position as a drawing-teacher and married Elisa, the daughter of a toy-maker, against his family's wishes. Then he left again, to travel, draw and study. This time he stopped in Chartres, where he spent ten days sketching every aspect of the cathedral. The young man's passion for those old stones grew ever deeper. He wrote long letters home: 'the rood screen is covered with figures which tell the world's most beautiful story [. . .] my eyes well up with tears and I wish my life would end right here in the rose window's light.'[1] His father, having managed to interest King Louis-Philippe in commissioning two watercolours from Eugène, financed an eighteen-month tour of Italy, so that his son could continue the education he had chosen for himself through drawing and studying architecture in situ. It was agreed that Elisa and their newborn baby would join him at some point in his Italian peregrinations. Sicily, Naples, Pompeii and Rome, where Eugène felt 'total stupefaction', educated him further in the art of architecture. The painter Ingres, then head of the Académie de France in Rome, received the young Viollet-le-Duc and his wife and drew a beautiful portrait of Elisa in lead pencil.

Not having followed the traditional path to becoming an architect, Eugène felt doubtful and nervous. What should he study next: physics, geometry, the mathematics of construction? In Venice he was attracted to the Middle Ages, in Florence to the Pitti Palace and the cathedral of Santa Maria del Fiore. Back in Paris, he resumed his teaching position, but something was gnawing at him: when would he be given a chance to demonstrate his architectural skills? He didn't have to wait long. His talent and passion had caught the eyes of powerful architects and publishers, who advertised his work and recommended him in high places.

The breakthrough came in 1838 when Mérimée hired Eugène, then twenty-four, in his Department of Historic

Monuments and gave him his first mission in Narbonne, in the south-west of France, before trusting him with the restoration of the basilica at Vézelay. What Mérimée and the Commission for Historic Monuments looked for in an architect was a critical eye as well as the scientific ability to assess what was required for a monument's restoration. They were not interested in people who would just patch up old buildings.

By 'restoration', Mérimée, and indeed Viollet-le-Duc, didn't mean repairing. They meant the act of unveiling and revealing the essence and original character of those monuments.[2] Restoration was in many ways an archaeological process, and often discoveries about the old structure and building would shed light on its original form and how, in later years, it had been misunderstood and mutilated. This was particularly true of medieval monuments. And this is probably why, after each work of restoration he did, Viollet-le-Duc felt compelled immediately to communicate his experience and his findings in journals. Between 1844 and 1846 he published eight articles in *Annales archéologiques*, from 'On the Construction of Religious Edifices since the Beginning of Christianity to the Sixteenth Century' to 'Building Vaults in the Thirteenth Century'.[3]

During those exciting first few years under the directorship of Mérimée, touring the country and going from one site to another, Viollet-le-Duc was also learning on the job how to supervise a building site, with its dozens, sometimes hundreds, of workers, its administration, financial management, accountancy, tendering procedures, regulations, necessary knowledge of all the materials used and validation of expenditures.

He had befriended an architect seven years his senior, Jean-Baptiste Lassus, and together they decided to present the Commission for Historic Monuments with a project for the restoration of Notre-Dame, which included the construction of a new spire (the last one, deemed too unstable, had been taken down in 1792). The fruit was ripe. Thanks to Victor Hugo's *Notre-Dame de Paris*, public opinion supported such costly and long restoration campaigns; people even demanded them from their government.

Viollet-le-Duc and Lassus's friendship with Prosper Mérimée probably helped: the commission greatly appreciated the restraint and simplicity of their project, which did not, however, lack the required ambition. It was also minutely detailed and well researched and, equally importantly, financially sound. Favoured over four other applications, their project, consisting of forty-four pages and twenty-two large-scale drawings, was officially chosen in March 1844, and the 30-year-old Viollet-le-Duc and 37-year-old Lassus were declared the competition's laureates.

Notre-Dame's restoration would take twenty years and span three different political regimes, from monarchy to republic and empire. All thanks to Mérimée, who, in order to safeguard his department, embraced each time the new political cause *du jour*. In 1851, a year before Louis-Napoleon turned the Second Republic into the Second Empire through a coup d'état, he wrote to Mérimée assuring him: 'Viollet-le-Duc can go about his business, I'll see that he doesn't get disturbed.'[4] In 1853 Mérimée became a senator so he could protect his army of architects. Remarkably, Viollet-le-Duc's grand restoration of Notre-Dame would not suffer from France's political upheavals. Louis-Napoleon, and perhaps Providence, seemed to have seen to it.

*

Viollet-le-Duc was three when an old servant first took him to visit Notre-Dame:

> He was carrying me in his arms for the cathedral was crowded. I suddenly saw the stained-glass south rose window and I just stared at it. The sun's rays were giving it an incredible glow. I can still remember where we were standing in the cathedral. And then the Grand Organ started playing. For me, as a small child, it was the stained-glass window that was singing. The old man was telling me that it was the organ but no, it was obviously the rose window. I attributed high-pitched notes to certain stained-glass panels, while others had a lower voice. I was soon terrified and he had to take me out.[5]

Viollet-le-Duc concluded: 'It is not education that gives us this intimate relationship with the arts.'

What was Viollet-le-Duc and Lassus's diagnosis in 1843 when they set off to restore Notre-Dame to her original magnificence? According to them, the twelfth- and thirteenth-century construction had been barbarically altered from the sixteenth century up to the early nineteenth century. Maurice de Sully's cathedral represented the 'core', therefore Notre-Dame at her most precious and pure. The 'casing' added in the late thirteenth century and throughout the fourteenth century had not, however, compromised the 'core', and had not clouded the overall clarity that was Notre-Dame.[6] In other words, three centuries had perfected Maurice de Sully's masterpiece, while another three centuries obscured it. Viollet-le-Duc and Lassus were committed to redressing those 300 years' worth of injuries.

They wanted, for instance, to give Notre-Dame back the thirteen steps that used to lead to her façade and had been filled in around 1507. They wished to restore the original statuary, either destroyed by time or by man, and in particular the gargoyles, which had almost all been replaced by ordinary lead pipes, not only represented the essence of Gothic art but also performed the role of drain pipes. They suggested putting back in place the stained glass above the nave and choir windows which the chapter's priests had destroyed in 1741 and 1753 and replaced with cheap, colourless glass. They also proposed to restore the tympanum of the central portal featuring the Last Judgment, which the architect Jacques-Germain Soufflot had simply cut down in 1771 to allow processions to enter the cathedral more easily. And then there was the spire.

The young architects also hoped to come across archaeological remnants which would supply new information about the cathedral's history and construction, and therefore help them better and more authentically redress the mutilations of the recent past.

While the National Assembly was voting on a special budget of 2.6 million francs for the first part of the restoration, the architects' two top priorities when they started work in spring 1845 were the façade and the statuary. Viollet-le-Duc had spent days and nights at Notre-Dame inspecting her every corner, trying to unmask and identify remnants of medieval imagery in order to reproduce them. Experts and artists had joined forces and taken to their drawing boards to sketch grimaces and faces that told 'stories'. The portals of the Virgin Mary and Saint Anne also needed to become 'legible' again. As for the twenty-eight kings of Judah, which had been wrongly thought of as kings of France and therefore beheaded during the revolution in 1793, the architects intended to place them all back into their empty niches on the façade's upper gallery.

Where the stone was in too dire a condition they replaced it, but on the whole, and rather remarkably, they scrupulously kept the original. Of the thirty-nine columns' capitals on the façade, for instance, only seven were replaced. Close inspection revealed traces of polychromy. This meant that the façade had originally been scattered with striking colours such as red and yellow, confirming what Viollet-le-Duc had long thought about the use of colour in medieval architecture. He had, in fact, always distinguished between medieval architecture, where structure and shape were not only revealed but often enhanced by colour, and Renaissance architecture, where painting was too often, in his eyes, merely used as 'furnishing colouring'. For him, paint was 'a sorceress': 'With one brush stoke it could destroy a well-conceived work, but it could also make a modest edifice sing.'[7]

On Notre-Dame's façade, Viollet-le-Duc had carefully studied the traces of paint he had uncovered on the columns' capitals and also on the blind arcade of the twenty-eight kings' niches; he concluded that, along with bright red, green and yellow, the colour black had played an important role: 'it lined the convex moulding, filled in backgrounds, surrounded ornaments, rede-signed shapes in large brushstrokes'.[8] Even though he was convinced that colour had covered parts of the façade, among others the kings of Judah's niches and the tympanums and arches of the portals, Viollet-le-Duc did not, however, suggest restoring Notre-Dame's colourful medieval features. Perhaps because he knew that there was no provision for decoration in national restoration budgets.

Instead, he produced a series of colourful patterns and sugges-tions for the chapels inside the cathedral, and it would be down to the Church and Notre-Dame's parishioners to pay for them if they so wished. Private donations started pouring in and many chapels in the nave and choir were thus painted. Following his recommendations, his young colleague the artist Auguste Perrodin painted blue and golden starry canopies, while walls in lighter shades were covered with colourful heraldic numbers. Viollet-le-Duc was delighted with the result: 'I never thought we could today find again this simplicity of lines, those trans-parent colours the recipe for which Italian monks seemed to have for ever buried in their cloisters.'[9]

Elsewhere in the cathedral, they started taking off all the layers of whitewash and crude white coats hastily given over the centuries each time Notre-Dame had needed to look good. Restoring the stained glass of the rose windows was also another priority, and to answer the clergy's needs Viollet-le-Duc and Lassus had been asked to build a new sacristy on the south flank of the cathedral, linked to the choir by a passage. Notre-Dame was France's biggest restoration site; however, five years later, in 1850, the architects had to pause: there wasn't any money left in the coffers. The legislators would have to vote and allocate more funds.

*

Thanks to Notre-Dame, Viollet-le-Duc's reputation had considerably grown and he was entrusted with an increasing number of commissions in France. He spent his time travelling and hardly saw his family – not that he seemed to care much, consumed as he was by his passion for old stones. The family adjusted to his absence, his lovely wife Elisa finding solace in the arms of the writer Charles Augustin Sainte-Beuve. Sainte-Beuve seems to have made a speciality of consoling dejected wives: he had just had a seven-year affair with Victor Hugo's wife Adèle when he turned his attention to Elisa.

Viollet-le-Duc's love for the Middle Ages and in-depth knowledge of Gothic art in particular meant that he became the go-to restorer of choice for medieval monuments. He was called to Carcassonne, to Saint-Denis and Saint-Sernin near Toulouse, among other places. The Second Republic (1848–52) came and went, slowing down slightly the pace of work due to political uncertainty and budget cuts. However, Prosper Mérimée had seen the future and had banked on Louis-Napoleon early enough, in other words before the coup d'état of 2 December 1851, in order to be able to keep his department running and his architects protected.

France's medieval monuments, six or seven centuries old, had reached a critical age and called for exhaustive renovation. Out of 2,400 listed buildings, 1,500 demanded urgent repairs, amounting to almost all the annual provision of 800,000 francs in 1848. Local authorities were not rich enough to allocate a special sum for their old monuments, so it was down to the government to foot the whole bill. And there were other, more recent monuments which also needed attention, such as the Louvre, for which French deputies voted an initial allocation of two million francs out of the twenty-five million needed. Three thousand workers were hired for the Louvre's rejuvenation. In fact, Mérimée knew that Louis-Napoleon would be sensitive to the argument that his department was employing thousands of workers, artisans and artists throughout France, thus creating a national educational and artisanal programme benefiting the whole economy. Mass employment was an essential part of Louis-Napoleon's plan to tame the restlessly insurrectional spirit of his compatriots.

In 1851, Viollet-le-Duc wrote a long article in the *Revue générale de l'architecture et des travaux publics* in order to convince public opinion and its representatives in parliament of the importance of continuing Notre-Dame's restoration, and thus grant it more public money. He recounted the nasty surprises they had found after stripping the walls of the *cache-misères* – coats of paint, bits of masonry and plastering – applied through centuries: large cracks in the façade, buttresses covered in saltpetre, the oxidation and porosity of the terraces, the rotten cornices behind the plaster fillers. The message was clear and emotional: Notre-Dame might be France's biggest and costliest restoration project, but it was badly needed!

Louis-Napoleon heard his plea. A special fund of six million francs would swiftly be voted for Notre-Dame. The French ruler would, however, test his architect's mettle. He decided on a Te Deum at the cathedral for New Year's Day 1852 and gave Viollet-le-Duc six days to dress up Our Lady.

Toiling night and day, hundreds of artisans and workers followed the architect's orders. In such a short time there was only one way of doing it: Viollet-le-Duc had chosen to expertly drape and artistically cover the work in progress. After removing the scaffolding from the façade, a crimson velarium spangled with golden stars was placed above the portals, welcoming the guests. Inside the cathedral, the south rose window was covered with light-blue silk embroidered with more golden stars, while huge trophies of flags played their part in the *trompe l'oeil* ensemble, hiding France's biggest building site. Columns had also been wrapped with gold-fringed, ruby-red silk velvet. Garlands of green foliage ran from column to column, circling the nave, while hundreds of candelabra supported 13,000 burning candles.[10]

Louis-Napoleon was so satisfied with the result that he chose the cathedral for his marriage to Eugénie de Montijo, a Spanish princess, on 30 January 1853. This time he asked Viollet-le-Duc for a decor worthy of Napoleon's coronation. An early daguerreotype showed the pop-up Gothic portico designed by the architects. It ran along the façade and featured equine statues of Charlemagne and Napoleon. More remarkably, four immense eagles seemed to be sitting on the cathedral's two towers, while tricolour and golden banners were hanging from the belfry. Inside, a profusion of flowers and draperies, silken veils, tapestries, banners, flags, carpets and canopies embroidered with golden bees, the Napoleonic symbol, completely hid the restoration work in progress and gave the cathedral the look of a jewel box. The bride, who was covered in diamonds, and the groom, in his lieutenant-general's uniform, were reportedly delighted. At 6 a.m. on the day after the ceremony the workers were back, and so was Viollet-le-Duc.

When Lassus suddenly died in 1857, Viollet-le-Duc was left alone to finish Notre-Dame's restoration and design the new spire. The French emperor gave his approval for the plans in March 1858. The old spire, in fact a small bell tower, was not deemed big enough – especially in comparison with that of nearby Sainte-Chapelle – to be replicated identically. Much attention was paid to what a future spire would look like against Paris's skyline. Spires had been a form of visual punctuation in medieval times, and Viollet-le-Duc had this in mind when he set out to draw the new *flèche*. He also wanted to use modern engineering to improve both the stability and the balance of the structure. The new spire would rest on the four piles of the transept. Octagonal in shape, its eight corner posts would in fact bend slightly inwards, in order for 'the eye to move, unhindered, from the spire's base to the apex above'. At its base, he imagined a series of 3-metre-high statues in wrought copper representing the twelve apostles and four evangelists, aligned as on Jacob's ladder. On top of the corner posts, long pinnacles formed the star-shaped base of the summit, decorated with folded wing eagles. The spire's framework, covered in lead, was scattered with gargoyles serving as a drainage system. Finally, at the very top, above the weathervane, stood a rooster sheltering in his copper entrails the relics of Saint Genevieve, the patron saint of Paris. The construction of the spire began on 14 February 1858 and was completed in the winter of 1860. Until the night of 15 April 2019, Viollet-le-Duc's spire was an emblem of Paris, a symbol of unity for France. Or, in the words of chief architect Pierre-Antoine Gatier, who is now in charge of the Eiffel Tower: 'It is a marker, a pointed finger, France's beating heart'.[11]

*

For all his love of medieval stones, Viollet-le-Duc was also a committed modern architect. For him, both concepts were actually linked, and he wanted future generations of French architects to embrace modernity through an in-depth knowledge of history, and especially the art of the thirteenth century. He wanted them to study it 'the same way one learns one's own language, in order to understand not only the words but also its grammar and its spirit'. For Viollet-le-Duc, ancient Greece and Rome belonged to the discipline of archaeology, while thirteenth-century French architecture offered the first lessons in art.[12] He campaigned passionately for students at the École des Beaux-Arts and the Académie de France to *study* rather than *imitate* the medieval style.

In architectural journals, but also in more accessible art publications such as the *Gazette des Beaux-Arts*, Viollet-le-Duc explained, for instance, the genius of the medieval architect Villard de Honnecourt (1200–50), whose sketchbooks had been republished in France in 1860. For Viollet-le-Duc, those admirable drawings showed what an architect should be: an engineer, an inventor, a land surveyor, a geometrician, a draughtsman, but also someone capable of 'doing a lot with little money', of leading teams of workers, negotiating prices, debating and interacting with landlords or bishops.

Throughout his life, Viollet-le-Duc fought the prejudices of his contemporaries against Gothic art. His sudden death in 1879, while working on the restoration of Lausanne cathedral in Switzerland, triggered eulogies to the man who had had no mentor, who had learnt his skills by himself in close contact with the works of the past. Many tributes insisted that he had opened up a new way, a new era for architects. His legacy included his *Dictionnaire* and his many *Entretiens*, or 'Conversations', and hundreds of scientific articles as well as, of course, his work of restoration.

Soon, though, his work and legacy were pilloried. Criticism came first from artists and writers such as John Ruskin, Marcel Proust and Auguste Rodin, whose love and appreciation of the Middle Ages was of another order. Poetic and symbolic, their enthusiasm in many ways opposed the spirit of Viollet-le-Duc's rationalist work and principles. In other words, they didn't speak the same language. After the First World War, artists condemned the very idea that thirteenth-century art and architecture could simply be restored through copying or casting it. Viollet-le-Duc became in their eyes nothing more than a forger. It is ironic, of course, that he should be considered as a neo-Gothic counterfeiter when what he did was to borrow from the medieval master builders their methods, not their models. To make matters worse for his legacy in France, between the 1930s and the 1970s Gothic art was looked down on, and Romanesque art considered superior for its simplicity.

It was in the 1980s that Viollet-le-Duc regained his stature and prestige in the eyes of art historians and architects, thanks both to new research on nineteenth-century art and architecture and also to an important exhibition at the Grand Palais which displayed the many facets of Viollet-le-Duc's genius, passion, knowledge and talent. However, in wider French society his name has largely remained synonymous with neo-medieval silliness. At least five generations were brought up to believe that the faux-Gothic style à la Viollet-le-Duc, also known in France as Henri II style, was inauthentic. In fact, Viollet-le-Duc's work is still being confused with that of poor-quality pastiche artists who fed the Gothic fad during the nineteenth century. And prejudices die hard.

*

After the fire of 15 April and in the middle of the Gilets Jaunes crisis, this bias against Viollet-le-Duc nourished a toxic national debate about the reconstruction of Notre-Dame's spire. French media set the scene for yet another potentially traumatic national rift, pitting the ancients against the moderns, that is the people in favour of rebuilding the spire as Viollet-le-Duc had designed it versus those who prefer that some twenty-first-century touch be added. Luckily for the nation's nerves, the heated debate quietened down as architects and workers on the ground focused on stabilizing the cathedral.

The issue will, however, return after chief architect Philippe Villeneuve delivers his diagnostic assessment to the French president. 'I am going to make proposals to the president and for

each I will present the pros and cons, but I am not the deci-
sion-maker. All I can say is that Notre-Dame is unique and
doesn't resemble any other Gothic cathedral.'[13] What about the
(perhaps unwise) five-year target for the reconstruction set by
Emmanuel Macron the day after the fire? 'In five years we can
rebuild the vaults and the roof, and reopen the church to both
worshippers and public. But nothing much more,' he warns.

Personally, he is not in favour of what he calls a *flèche signature*, in other words a trophy spire. In the 850 years of the
cathedral's existence, every architect who built or restored
Notre-Dame has served the monument rather than himself. The
first four architects, in other words the cathedral's 'authors',
remain anonymous. We don't know who they were, and they
most probably wouldn't have considered themselves as anything
other than builders.

Viollet-le-Duc himself succeeded in blending his work with
the original medieval architecture. For Villeneuve, 'Viollet-Le-
Duc's great talent lies in the fact that his work was almost
indiscernible from that of the medieval builders. His spire was
not identifiable; it could well have dated back to the thirteenth
century.' In fact, many art historians consider that Notre-Dame
is as much a work of the thirteenth century as it is of the nineteenth-century reinvention. Yet Viollet-le-Duc also discreetly
used the latest technical innovations and inspired many of his
younger colleagues. Indeed, the Statue of Liberty was conceived
on the roof of Notre-Dame: Viollet-Le-Duc had used a sophis-
ticated metallic structure covered in wrought copper for the
statues of the spire which Auguste Bartholdi copied for his
monument in New York.

The Dutch architect Rem Koolhaas, professor of architecture and urban design at Harvard University's Graduate School of Design, was four in 1948, when his grandfather took him to Paris for the first time. They went from museums to cafés and from cafés to more Parisian landmarks: 'I was in awe. Once at Notre-Dame, my granddad showed and explained to me every part of the cathedral so the place became familiar. I returned to it every time I came to Paris, as a routine and a ritual.'[14] Later, as a young teenager, he read Victor Hugo's *Notre-Dame de Paris*. 'I saw how Notre-Dame was an emblem as well as a real provocation, an assertion of modernity. How could something as ancient be so modern?' How did he judge the flurry of projects for a new spire that sprang up in the hours following the fire? He found it hard to understand. 'A contemporary gesture is not called for. It is in fact crucial to maintain Viollet-le-Duc's remarkable work and thinking. I am optimistic, though; I am sure France will treat Notre-Dame with integrity.'

Let us light a candle.

8

1865

Haussmann 'Unclutters' the Île de la Cité

'Like an elephant in the middle of a desert.'

Pierre-Marie Auzas[1]

To be alive, in Paris, during the Second Empire! Louis-Napoleon had none of the genius of his uncle, Napoleon Bonaparte, but he certainly was shrewd and knew a thing or two about his compatriots. Remarkably for a man who preferred London, which he knew far better, having lived there in exile for much of his early life, to Paris, Louis-Napoleon arguably made more impact on the French capital city than any other ruler since the Middle Ages. Having secured his power with, first of all, a simulacrum of democratic institutions, secondly, a seemingly tolerant system of censorship (which relied on self-censorship), and thirdly, the spending of huge amounts of public money, Louis-Napoleon kept dazzling the French, and especially Parisians, for he thought that was the best way to rein them in. He would lavishly 'modernize' the country and its capital, and tame its insurrectional spirit with state-sponsored mass employment.

He struck a radically different figure from Louis-Philippe, 'the citizen king' of the 1830s and 1840s, who did everything he could to avoid royal extravaganza and appear as a 'king of the people', or a *'roi bourgeois'* as the French called it. Dressing down was, for instance, a requisite, and he could be seen in elegant but rather simple attire walking on the Parisian boulevards with a very small entourage. Louis-Napoleon went in the opposite direction: nothing was too magnificent for him and for France. The concept of *nouveau-riche* could have been invented for him. Central to his power was the issue of his succession. When his wife Eugénie gave birth to a male heir in 1856, Notre-Dame was naturally chosen for the christening ceremony. It was of paramount political importance that the young Napoleon Eugène, known to his parents as Loulou, be consecrated and introduced as the next natural ruler. A set of four new bells, Angélique-Françoise, Antoinette-Charlotte, Hyacinthe-Jeanne and Denise-David, were immediately ordered for the event, and it was decided that the decor created by Eugène Viollet-le-Duc and Jean-Baptiste Lassus for Louis-Napoleon and Eugénie's wedding three years earlier befitted the imperial occasion.

Loulou's godfather was Pope Pius IX, his godmother the queen of Sweden, but they were represented respectively by Cardinal Vicar Constantino Patrizi and the Grand Duchess of Baden. A sign, perhaps, that they didn't quite take this new French dynasty so seriously. Following his motto of living on credit, Louis-Napoleon borrowed 400,000 francs to finance the celebration. For the event, the emperor gave twelve sumptuous sets of white silk copes, tunics, chasubles and stoles to the chapter. The clergy attended en masse, with eighty-five arch-bishops and bishops standing in the choir, while another 5,000 guests had been invited to the nine-month-old's baptism.

*

Viollet-le-Duc had already been working tirelessly on Notre-Dame's restoration for ten years when Baron Haussmann was chosen by Louis-Napoleon to redesign Paris. Apart from the cathedral, which was about to be reborn in new Gothic splen-dour, Paris was a mess. Or, as Rupert Christiansen puts it in *City of Light*, 'the fabric of the place was in a dismal state of decay; its oases of splendour such as the Louvre or the Arc de Triomphe surrounded by a foetid wilderness of filth, stench and crime, pitted with noxious warrens of tortuous backstreets cramped with decrepit tenement housing and swarms of wretched humanity'.[2]

In just sixty-five years its population had more than tripled, from 547,000 in 1801 to 1,800,000 in 1866. And this despite two major outbreaks of cholera in 1832 and 1849, which had together cost the lives of more than 20,000 people. Parisian traf-fic was notoriously hellish and daily congestion hindered the capital's economic activity. There were also questions of public health, blocked sewers, lack of public lighting – all issues which needed to be urgently addressed, and which could not be indef-initely postponed. There had been attempts at remapping the city under Louis XVI, the revolution, the First Empire and Louis-Philippe. Napoleon had constructed the arcaded rue de Rivoli, linking place de la Concorde to Châtelet, and the Comte de Rambuteau, the prefect of the Seine department, had built new sewers and water conduits in some parts of the Right Bank, but these were limited and isolated efforts and partial answers to much deeper and bigger interconnected problems.

It was time for a radical and comprehensive vision of Paris. The development of the railways, with their stations right in the heart of the capital, added extra pressure to create clear routes of communication. The cost of redesigning the French capital, which entailed a massive programme of demolition, expropriation and compensation, promised to be astronomical. At first, the municipality baulked at such a prospect: where would they find the money? Louis-Napoleon stepped in: the money would be borrowed from the banks, and a legal process for expropriation, offering generous financial terms but no chance of appeal, was voted for by legislators. To oversee such a big scheme, Louis-Napoleon needed a right-hand man. He found him in Bordeaux.

Georges-Eugène Haussmann, of Protestant Alsatian origin, had excelled as prefect of Bordeaux: sharp, efficient, hard-working, disciplined, organized and without any political ambition. An opera enthusiast and amateur cellist, he had nonetheless chosen to study law. He cut a dashing figure: tall, handsome, broad-shouldered. However, he lacked charm. He was direct to the point of appearing blunt and had little patience with protocol. He was there to get things done. Appointed prefect of the Seine, Haussmann began the job immediately, on 29 June 1853, and would stick to a daily routine of starting work at 6 a.m. Louis-Napoleon had given him the general idea: 'cut through the city's clogged arteries and allow it to breathe more freely'.[3] Whenever Louis-Napoleon was in Paris, they would meet daily.

Historians have often pointed to his having had to battle asthma attacks in filthy Paris in his youth to understand Haussmann's peculiar interest in opening up – others would say butchering – Paris with the unsentimental precision of a surgeon. He first began with place du Carrousel (where the Louvre Pyramid currently stands), which was cluttered with crumbling tenements and stables, the sight of which he had always thought shameful. Next came the *grande croisée*, the great crossroads with Châtelet as its epicentre. Gare du Nord and Gare de l'Est would be linked directly through a series of boulevards to the southern tip of Paris. As for rue de Rivoli, it would be extended eastwards to Bastille. Completed in 1859, the large north–south and east–west thoroughfares with their gorgeous, wide, tree-lined pavements were greeted with joy by Parisians. Air at last.

Through the 1860s, a further 26 kilometres of boulevards were created around all the different train stations, and big squares, or *places*, such as that around the Arc de Triomphe, were redesigned with avenues symmetrically leading off them. On the Left Bank boulevard Saint-Germain was extended eastwards, triggering the demolition of splendid *hôtels particuliers* (private mansions), sacrificed to rational thinking and straight lines. The area around the Panthéon was drastically altered too, but it was the Île de la Cité that underwent the most thorough reinvention – and thus demolition.

Haussmann hated the Île de la Cité. His aversion was the stuff of childhood nightmares. 'As a sickly asthmatic child repelled by dirt and terrified of foul air, he had traumatically been obliged to cross the Île from his home to school every morning.'[4] The exterminator of squalor and filth, the enemy of damp and crime, Haussmann would eradicate almost all of the island's medieval flesh and spirit, bar Notre-Dame, Sainte-Chapelle, the Conciergerie and parts of the sixteenth-century place Dauphine.

Two new bridges, pont Saint-Michel and pont au Change, provided more crossing points. The Hôtel-Dieu hospital and the orphanage of *enfants perdus*, standing right on the edge of the island's south flank, were demolished to be rebuilt further north of the parvis, the idea being to unclutter the surroundings of the cathedral: no more shacks. Besides, Haussmann wanted people walking on the Left Bank to have a clear view of Notre-Dame from the west, south and east. It was a view that came at a human price.

Two charmless and imposing new buildings, the police prefecture opposite Notre-Dame and the Tribunal de Commerce on the site of a theatre near Sainte-Chapelle, were responsible for the expulsion of thousands of working-class Parisians. Before Haussmann's intervention, around 15,000 people inhabited the Île de la Cité. When he finished its redesign, only 5,000 Parisians still called the island their home.[5] Haussmann had had his revenge, and one could certainly now breathe freely there; but nowhere else in Paris had he been so brutal. Did he ever regret it? In 1970, lines on the parvis were traced out in light-coloured cobblestones to show where the rue Neuve of medieval times had once run. A way, perhaps, to heal the island's wounded memory.

In the collective imagination, Haussmann has been put on trial many times for what he did to Paris. However, we are also heavily indebted to him for the new, dazzling and salubrious capital city he gave us, for the large boulevards, the beautiful *places*, the parks of Buttes-Chaumont and Montsouris, for the Opéra Garnier, the Halles Baltard and a vast sewerage system comprising 60 kilometres of gaslit tunnels which every foreign head of state asked to visit upon their completion.

Haussmann did indeed devastate a whole community, but one mostly living off petty crime and prostitution and sleeping in dilapidated shacks infested with disease; he single-mindedly demolished a medieval past that had been romanticized by Victor Hugo's *Notre-Dame de Paris*, but also cleaned up what were foetid backstreets. And if Notre-Dame has now stood in lonely majesty at the tip of the Île de la Cité for 150 years, visible to all, from west to south and south to east, it is thanks to Baron Haussmann.

For centuries, Notre-Dame had lived in symbiosis with Parisians, enshrouded in shambles, ensconced in the tumult of life. Suddenly she stood isolated yet magnificent, facing an immense square, 150 metres wide and 200 metres long, six times its medieval size. The late nineteenth century completely changed the way the cathedral interacted with her environment and the way in which people now saw her.

Baron Haussmann was as much a demolisher as a stage director. He displayed Notre-Dame, for some critics 'like an elephant in the middle of a desert', for others as the jewel in Paris's crown for everyone to admire and possess. It was thanks to Baron

Haussmann that Notre-Dame could now be appreciated in her integrity by anyone who set eyes on her. 'Thanks to Haussmann, Notre-Dame became more readable, more visible, she became whole.'[6]

9

1944

De Gaulle at the Liberation

'The Magnificat rises. Has it ever been more ardently sung?
However, shooting continues inside.'[1]

When war broke out in September 1939, the Third Republic had ruled over France for sixty-nine years. Since the French Revolution France had known eight different political regimes, of which the Third Republic had proved the longest and most resilient. Not for long, though. It had only a few months to live.

However, the Third Republic has forever left its mark on France's DNA through the 1905 Law on the Separation of Church and State. This law, which tore families apart, has had a profound impact on French society. In the second half of the nineteenth century, a strong anti-clerical sentiment became the trademark of republicanism. The 1905 law heralded a new wave of free thinking and emancipation from the tutelage of the Church in every aspect of French life; it offered an exhilarating feeling of freedom of conscience for the majority of French citizens. However, even as the clergy became the subject of constant mockery and a favourite topic for France's notoriously virulent satire, the cathedral of Notre-Dame, although a place of worship, remained above the fray and beyond criticism. 'The republic feigns to disregard this great body it both admires and fears. In fact, it finds in Notre-Dame a recourse in its moments of despair, attempting then to plead with a God it likes to ignore but whom it implores.'[2]

As piles of protective sandbags were placed in Notre-Dame's every portal and door, in the stalls of the choir and around its most precious statues inside the nave, just as they had been in the First World War, Cardinal Emmanuel Suhard became archbishop of Paris. He, like other Parisians, would watch, powerless, the arrival in the city of the Germans on 14 June 1940 after a blitzkrieg in which the Wehrmacht invaded the north of France in just a few weeks, which neither British nor French forces had been able to stop. The French premier, Paul Reynaud, declared Paris an open city on 11 June as he and the government prepared to flee to Tours and then Bordeaux. Before leaving, Reynaud made the American ambassador, William Christian Bullitt, in effect governor of Paris.

The American community in Paris, the largest in continental Europe,[3] had nourished a special relationship with the city ever since the French Revolution, when the National Assembly had ordered three days of national mourning to honour the death of Benjamin Franklin, one of the Founding Fathers of the United States. It must have felt almost natural that the American ambassador, the last diplomat to remain in occupied Paris, should represent its interests. The 49-year-old Bullitt, a former news correspondent in Europe, American ambassador in Soviet

Russia between 1933 and 1936, a man of the world with a penchant for beautiful women, was an ardent European. He was also perfectly trilingual, thanks to his mother, Louisa Horwitz, herself of German and Jewish origin and who knew that languages were the best of gifts.

Just before leaving on 12 June, unsure as he was that the Germans would abide by international conventions of war by which open cities should be protected from bombing, Reynaud had begged his friend Bullitt to persuade the Wehrmacht not to destroy Paris. After bidding farewell to Reynaud, Bullitt asked to be driven to Notre-Dame cathedral. There he attended a prayer service led by Cardinal Suhard. 'Kneeling in the front pew, he was seen to weep for the city and country he loved.'[4] Was he praying for strength, or for a miracle?

With renewed resolve, Bullitt sent his military and naval attachés to meet the German general commander. At first it was agreed that German forces would enter the city peacefully; however, the shooting of Nazi officers by French *résistants* near Porte Saint-Denis enraged the German 18th Army commander, General Georg von Küchler, so much that he ordered an all-out air and artillery assault on Paris at eight o'clock the following morning. Bullitt had only a few hours left to save Paris from Nazi destruction, of the kind recently suffered by Warsaw and Rotterdam. His fluent German and French proved vital: he sent two French officials to meet their German counterparts in the town of Écouen, 18 kilometres north of Paris, to settle the terms of the handover. Küchler relented and signed the relevant documents, calling off the bombardment of Paris. An American had saved the City of Light.

Then the German occupiers turned Paris into stone. 'Was there not some Greek myth about the man who tried to ravish the goddess, only to have her turn to stone when he touched her? That is really what happened to Paris. When the Germans came, the soul simply went out of it; and what is left is stone,'[5] wrote the 36-year-old American diplomat George F. Kennan in his diary on 3 July 1940.

For four years Paris looked as if it had fallen into a deep sleep; but for those who could hear it, its heart was still beating. At Notre-Dame, religious services and ceremonies continued. On 18 May 1941 a votive lamp of the perpetual rosary was fixed at the feet of the fourteenth-century statue of Notre-Dame de Paris. It would burn night and day until the liberation. Almost exactly three years later, on 21 May 1944, as preparations for the D-Day landings were getting under way, public prayers for the soul of France were said at Notre-Dame: 25,000 Parisians participated from the parvis as the cathedral was too crowded. Cardinal Suhard led the service: 'Our Lady of Paris, Queen of France and Queen of Peace, listen to us! Listen to our prayers!'[6]

However, a few weeks later, on 2 July, Cardinal Suhard unwisely agreed to celebrate the funeral Mass of the staunch collaborationist Philippe Henriot, executed by a commando of *résistants* four days earlier. Representatives of Marshal Pétain's puppet government in Vichy, including Prime Minister Pierre Laval, were attending en masse alongside German officers in what would prove to be the last ignominious manifestation of Vichy France. While many priests had enrolled in the Resistance, Cardinal Suhard was better known for his all-too-neutral stance on politics. When, in August 1944, Paris started seething with insurrectional spirit, the Resistance asked the cardinal to make himself scarce: he should not fear for his life, but he should know that he was not wanted.

On 16 August the insurrection began. Radio Paris, the notorious pro-German radio station, suddenly stopped broadcasting, its leaders having vanished during the night. The fightback had started, but these times were fraught with danger. The Resistance, eager but badly equipped, did not have the military might needed to destroy the German forces stationed in the capital, especially their tanks. If it were to rise up too soon, Paris risked complete destruction and a bloodbath for its civilians.

The different factions of the Resistance were concerned about the time it would take the French 2nd Armoured Division, known as the 2nd DB, commanded by General Philippe Leclerc under the orders of General de Gaulle, to reach Paris. Besides, like all Free French forces that took part in the Normandy landings, the 2nd DB was ultimately under the American high command, which complicated things further. Despite de Gaulle's insistence, General Dwight Eisenhower was in two minds about diverting forces to liberate Paris: the fate of the French capital might have been of high symbolic importance but it was not a military priority. However, the Parisian *résistants*, Gaullists and Communists alike, mostly in their twenties, were all burning with impatience.

The general mobilization order was given on 18 August. Resistance posters had been pasted on every wall of the French capital the night before. It was a call to former officers and officer cadets and 'all able-bodied men and women to join the ranks' of the Resistance and 'strike the Germans and Vichy's traitors wherever they can be found'.[7] The uprising thus began at dawn on 19 August. Opposite Notre-Dame, two thousand armed French policemen locked themselves in the prefecture and started shooting at German soldiers and tanks. This set off the signal for the building of barricades at all strategic cross-roads, with the aim of hindering the mobility of German tanks. The FFI, the *résistants* of the Forces Françaises Intérieures, began occupying key buildings such as town halls, ministries, printing works and newspaper offices.

That day General Leclerc decided, in agreement with General de Gaulle but without American consent, to send a small advance party to Paris. On 21 August the Resistance's one-sheet newspapers, printed during the night, were exhorting Parisians to 'hold the siege and keep attacking the enemy in every possible way'. Albert Camus, editor of *Combat*, had found the right words: 'What is an insurrection? It is the people in arms. What is the people? It is those within a nation who will never kneel.'[8] On 22 August Eisenhower and General Omar Bradley, the American field commander, finally ordered the 4th Infantry Division to help Leclerc liberate Paris. The French Resistance now held half of Paris, but ammunition was getting scarce and Parisians were on the brink of famine.

As agreed between Eisenhower and de Gaulle, Leclerc's 2nd DB would enter Paris first. A small vanguard reached the square of the Hôtel de Ville at 9.20 p.m. on 24 August. An order was despatched to Notre-Dame to ring its bells. At 11.22 p.m. the then 258-year-old lowest-pitch bourdon of the Cathedral, Emmanuel, rang out in F sharp so loudly that it could be heard at least 8 kilometres away. The radio-operators of the newly established Radiodiffusion de la Nation Française had just called on priests to follow suit, and the bells of the city's churches began to accompany the deep voice of Notre-Dame's largest bell.

'The incredibly grave sounds booming out from Notre-Dame stunned us. With Notre-Dame's bells rose a more profound voice, which seemed to be saying: "Reflect, pay your respects, the moment is superb but it is also terrible," '[9] recalled the 35-year-old Gaullist writer and *résistant* Yves Cazaux in his diary.

On 25 August, as dawn broke over avenue d'Orléans,[10] which links the main southern gate of Paris with the Left Bank in a straight north–south line, Parisians were woken by tremors: every building shook as the tanks of the French 2nd Armoured Division roared past. Indoors, Parisians old and young jumped for joy, soon thronging the streets to greet their liberators. 'We could all feel our hearts beating as one. There were no civilians, there were no soldiers, there was one free people,'[11] wrote the 39-year-old philosopher Jean-Paul Sartre amid the multitude.

'For four years, Paris had been the free world's remorse. Suddenly it became its magnet,'[12] wrote Charles de Gaulle about those moments. The leader of the Free French knew that 'Paris would decide the question of power in France' – that is, if its American allies didn't interfere. De Gaulle, who had been greeted like a hero in the various towns of Brittany and Normandy through which he had travelled since the Normandy landings, knew that, unlike the British, the American administration was still in contact with Vichy and other louche so-called French representatives. Washington, wary of the French

Communist Party Resistance, was not completely convinced it should give de Gaulle free rein.

He knew, though, what needed to be done and that he had to reach Paris as soon as possible. 'What I need to do there: gather every soul into one national *élan*, but also immediately show and demonstrate the figure and authority of the state.'[13]

*

In the car that drove him to Paris on 25 August, de Gaulle felt 'full of both emotion and serenity'.[14] Just after 4 p.m. he reached Montparnasse train station, where General Leclerc presented him with the signed letter of surrender from General Dietrich von Choltitz, Hitler's representative in Paris, the ink still fresh. Everybody expected de Gaulle to go straight to the Hôtel de Ville. Instead he chose to head to the Ministry of War at 14 rue Saint Dominique, near the Invalides where Napoleon's tomb lies. The Ministry of War, the heart of France's new command and government, was where he should now be.

The last time he set foot in this early-eighteenth-century *hôtel particulier*, which was once inhabited by Napoleon's mother, was on the night of 10 June 1940 with Paul Reynaud. 'Not a piece of furniture, not a curtain, not a tapestry has been moved. On the minister's desk, the telephone is still in the same place. Am told this is the case in every ministry. Nothing has changed, nothing is lacking, except the state. I will put it back.'[15]

He faced two urgent priorities: public order and food supply. At 7 p.m. he went to the police prefecture to review the police troops. From there he walked with his aides through an exultant crowd across the parvis of Notre-Dame, and from rue d'Arcole and pont d'Arcole reached the Hôtel de Ville, where the National Council of the Resistance was waiting for him. Pressed to address the crowd, he improvised a speech, broadcast live by radio-operators:

> Why should we hide the overwhelming emotion that each of us feels here, at home, in a Paris that liberated itself? No! We won't bury this profound and sacred feeling. There are minutes that go beyond our poor lives. Paris! An outraged Paris! A broken Paris! A martyred Paris! But, a liberated Paris! . . . Since the enemy that held Paris has capitulated into our hands, France returns to Paris, to her home. She returns bloodstained, but resolute. She returns enlightened by immense lessons, but more certain than ever of her duties and of her rights.[16]

Many leaders of the Resistance asked him solemnly to proclaim the republic to the crowd, but he replied: 'The republic never ceased to exist. Free France, combative France, has incarnated the republic. Vichy France always was and remains null and void. I am myself the president of the government of the republic. Why would I go and proclaim it?'[17]

Back late at the Ministry of War, de Gaulle received the figures of the day's casualties and prisoners: 14,800 German prisoners, 3,200 German soldiers killed, 600 French soldiers and 28 officers of the 2nd DB dead. Those numbers would have to be added to the 2,500 French *résistants* killed since the beginning of the insurrection a week earlier and the 1,000 civilian casualties.[18]

General de Gaulle knew that only the people could crown a man. He had planned to show himself and gain their trust the following day, on the afternoon of 26 August. He would walk from the Arc de Triomphe to Notre-Dame, where he would listen to a Te Deum of victory. The Radiodiffusion de la Nation Française had been relaying the news on the wireless and, despite the lack of private and public transport, early-morning reports indicated that many inhabitants of the surrounding area, known as the Île de France, had started walking towards Paris to be there.

*

The 2nd DB stationed its tanks at the Arc de Triomphe, place de la Concorde and the parvis of Notre-Dame. Everybody was aware of the risks. The Luftwaffe had many planes left in the north of Paris and die-hard German snipers were still hiding in the capital. At 3 p.m. de Gaulle, surrounded by members of the French Resistance with guns on hips, gendarmes in uniform and even a bailiff with a golden chain around his neck, symbol of republican ritual, revived the flame at the grave of the unknown soldier for the first time since June 1940. 'It is like a dream finally realized,'[19] he later wrote in his memoirs.

Then he turned towards the Champs-Élysées. 'Ah! This is the sea! An immense crowd, perhaps two million souls. Roofs and windows are packed with people, they have climbed on every lamp-post, every mast and ladder available. As far as the eye can see, there is this human wave, under the sun, under the *tricolore*.'[20] De Gaulle walked down the Champs-Élysées, tall and calm. He knew the people were there for him. He symbolized their hope. He knew he must appear fraternal, approachable, the image of national unity. 'Many around me fear attacks from the enemy, but today I believe in France's fortune.'[21]

De Gaulle walked in the middle of an indescribably jubilant crowd chanting his name. 'At this instant in time, something is happening, one of those miracles of the national conscience, one of those gestures which sometimes, through the centuries, come and illuminate our history. In this community which is but one single thought, one single *élan*, one single chant, differences have vanished, individuals have disappeared.'[22] De Gaulle not only acknowledged the crowd with friendly gestures, he also saluted the statues of historical figures on his way, such as Georges Clémenceau, former prime minister of France during World War I, and Joan of Arc. He looked around, deeply aware of walking as if through French history, from the Champs-Élysées to place de la Concorde where the heads of Louis XVI and Marie-Antoinette fell, along the Tuileries and the Louvre thinking of Napoleon Bonaparte, to the Hôtel de Ville and the memory of the Commune. 'History, concentrated in these stones, in these streets, seems to be smiling today. It is also warning us.'[23]

In front of the Hôtel de Ville, under the eyes of American and British camera-operators, de Gaulle inspected troops. Images are important. He knew Washington would keenly scrutinize the newsreels.

The Te Deum at Notre-Dame, the day's climax, was scheduled at 5 p.m. but de Gaulle was early. The cathedral had been packed for hours, and many Parisians who arrived too late to get in chose to wait for the general either on the parvis or on pont d'Arcole and rue d'Arcole, linking the Hôtel de Ville on the Right Bank with the Île de la Cité.

On pont d'Arcole was 8-year-old Marguerite-Marie Peresson, who had come with her mother and blind father, 'who was adamant he had to be there'.[24] As she saw de Gaulle passing she exclaimed: 'Oh, how handsome he is!' Twelve years later, aged twenty, she would blush at the recollection. Still reeling from the emotion of having seen *le grand homme*, the little girl then heard gunshots going off in quick succession.

Everybody lay flat on the pavement and Marguerite-Marie's mother urged her to pray. Each time she looked up her mother pushed her head down to the ground, ordering her to keep praying. 'Never said so many Ave Marias in my life!' Marguerite-Marie later recalled.

Opposite the cathedral, on the parvis, standing with his wife and little boy, Georges Delarue, a veteran of the First World War, had noticed men on the upper gallery of the north tower of the cathedral and had been wondering who they were when he heard the crowd cheering de Gaulle coming from rue d'Arcole. Moments later he heard two gunshots, followed by riposte firing from the 2nd DB stationed on the parvis. 'This was an assassination attempt on de Gaulle, there was no doubt about that.'[25] Crouched behind their bicycles, Georges Delarue and his family slowly retreated across the Petit Pont towards the Left Bank and found refuge in a pharmacy on rue Saint-Jacques, where a lady covered in blood was soon brought in.

Mademoiselle Vésinet had been sitting near the front rows of Notre-Dame since 1.45 p.m. 'I simply wasn't going to miss this.' She chose to sit in the nave, at the front, on the first chair next to the aisle in order to see de Gaulle close up. Just after 4 p.m. she and the crowd in the cathedral heard some brouhaha outside the central portal, gunshots went off and the general appeared. 'He walked up the nave towards the altar. He looked so tranquil while the rest of us crouched and ducked, afraid of the shooting.' Shots were now fired from within the cathedral, from the upper gallery, near the Grand Organ. 'When we saw how imperturbable he was, unmoved by the commotion, we somehow resumed our position on the pews but shooting was still going on. It was the most surreal thing.' Cardinal Suhard, nowhere to be seen, had left his deputy and canons to greet de Gaulle. They showed him to the crimson presidential chair where he sat, next to the altar.

Twenty-seven-year-old Raymond Marcillac, a radio-operator and journalist, was carrying out his very first assignment and his first live-broadcast. He had arrived suitably early with his bulky equipment and had found a spot on the upper gallery with a panoramic view over the nave, near the choir, with a clear view of the assembly below. He started broadcasting as shots were fired. Here is an extract from his live report, delivered in a sometimes panting, gasping and crackling voice.[26] Marcillac was broadcasting lying flat on the floor of the upper gallery, close to the shooters:

[*Over sounds of heavy fire*] The courageous soldiers of General Leclerc will hopefully get those cowards who are firing at the crowd. General de Gaulle has now made his entrance [*sounds of gunshots and applause*]. The general is rearranging some chairs, he has miraculously escaped the attack. The general, very calm despite the commotion and the shooting, advances towards the choir. The sacristan shows him the presidential chair and I can say it [*sounds of gunshots*], and I will say it [*sounds of gunshots*], here in front of us is the president of the Republic. He seems completely unmoved by the hail of bullets, he is magnificent [*sounds of gunshots*]. People are taking refuge under their chairs, crouching. The canons have arrived despite the tumult and general commotion [*sounds of gunshots*]. The general seems oblivious; his sangfroid is remarkable. People are standing up again, going back to where they were sitting, cheering the general. The doors are now being closed. Order seems to have been restored by General Leclerc's men.

The sound of the Magnificat rose while sporadic shots could be heard inside and outside the cathedral. Raymond Marcillac confirmed it live on radio: 'While the assembly sings the Magnificat, I can see General Leclerc's men entering the cathedral to get the shooters still present in the cathedral [*sound of Magnificat being sung*]. The moment is exceptional. You cannot imagine the emotion for everyone here, trying not to show fear but only affection to the new leader of France.'

General de Gaulle may have looked calm and confident, but he knew he needed to bring the ceremony to a close, no matter how wonderful it felt: it was becoming too dangerous for the people who had come to see him. This is how he recalled those minutes:

The moment I arrive in front of Notre-Dame, shots are fired. It is crucial not to give in to the agitation. I therefore enter the cathedral where some shooting is also taking place. I walk towards the choir, people cheer, albeit crouched. I take my seat. Priests and canons are in the stalls. The Magnificat rises. Has it ever been more ardently sung? However, shooting continues inside. Bullets are ricocheting on the vaults and bits of masonry are falling on people's heads. I must end the ceremony after the Magnificat.[27]

De Gaulle stood up, people cheered and applauded him as he passed; some kissed his hands. As he exited the cathedral he exchanged a few words with Leclerc and was driven to his new home on rue Saint-Dominique. Later that day the Luftwaffe bombarded parts of Paris, destroying 500 houses and killing or injuring 1,000 civilians.[28] De Gaulle wrote: 'Tonight, after so much tumult, everything quietens around me. It is time to acknowledge what has just been accomplished and to face what is about to begin. Today, unity has prevailed.'[29]

10

2013

The Bells of Notre-Dame

This sonorous isle

Parisians learnt about it from reading *Le Parisien*[1] while having their breakfast on the morning of Palm Sunday, 24 March 2013. Later that day, at 6 p.m., Notre-Dame's brand-new bells would all ring together for the first time with the old bourdon Emmanuel, which had been hanging in the south tower since 1686. This was a historical and musical event not to be missed.

Families, together with almost one million tourists, had been able to see them close up in February. The bells, each around 2 metres in diameter, were exhibited in the nave of Notre-Dame for everyone to admire. After all, they would soon be moved up to the north and south towers and stay there for at least the next 300 years: better get a good look while one could.

Even the feminist militants FEMEN had been drawn to the nine shiny bells. On the afternoon of 12 February, eight young women wearing long black coats managed to sneak inside the cathedral without the crowd noticing. When they found themselves near enough, they suddenly jumped inside the security perimeter, flinging off their coats and appearing naked apart from black-satin *culottes*. And they started striking the bells with wooden sticks while shouting, 'Pope, no more!' They later said in court that they had meant to celebrate the recent and unexpected retirement of Pope Benedict XVI. The cathedral's security staff tried to cover them up before ushering them outside; one young woman unfortunately broke a tooth in the melee.

*

The nine bells arrived at the Île de la Cité on 31 January by *convoi exceptionnel*. Quietly aligned and expertly strapped onto an open double-truck crane trailer, the resplendent bronze bells left their foundry at Villedieu-les-Poêles in Normandy at dawn, travelling for four hours on the motorway before reaching the French capital. During their journey, French drivers hooted their horns in appreciation. From Paris's main western gate, Porte Maillot, Monsignor Patrick Jacquin, the cathedral's rector, perched on an open-top double-decker bus, and a police squadron on motorbikes escorted them to their final destination. The bells slowly rolled down the Champs-Élysées, passing the Louvre en route to Notre-Dame, applauded along the way by cheering, smiling crowds.

Bell-lovers, campanologists, musicians of all kinds had waited so long for this moment. To think that the cathedral's bells had not chimed in tune since 1769! Worse still: since 1856, four of them had been replaced by poorly executed substitutes, further straining sensitive ears each time they rang. Few Parisians knew or had even noticed. After all, how could they compare them with Notre-Dame's perfect timbre of 1769? They had simply got used to her disharmonious voice, like that of a beloved, creaky, old relative.

The French Revolution had been particularly unkind to the bells, of which there were originally twenty, distributed between the two towers and the spire. Their three-dimensional location, forming an isosceles triangle, and their elevation at different heights according to their weight and sonority gave them a particularly impressive depth of tone. In 1792, however, Notre-Dame sounded decidedly hoarse. Sixteen bells were removed to be melted and transformed into canon and coinage for the young republic. Only Emmanuel was spared, alongside three bells in the north tower.[2] And the spire with its little bells was eventually taken down for fear of its collapse. Eugène Viollet-le-Duc's magnificent renovations between 1844 and 1865 gave Notre-Dame back a spire, enchanting gargoyles, the gallery of kings of Judah on the façade and numerous other wondrous neo-medieval ornaments, but, strangely, the bells were not restored to their pre-revolutionary glory. It would take another 160 years.

For her 850th anniversary it was decided that Notre-Dame cathedral would buy herself a present and, for once, wouldn't ask the state for a penny. A sum of two million euros was raised privately to order a new set of nine bells from the best foundries in Europe.[3] The Cornille-Havard foundry at Villedieu-les-Poêles won the commission for eight bells while the Netherlands' royal Eijsbouts foundry based in Asten was chosen for the 'small' 6-tonne bourdon, Marie.[4]

At Villedieu-les-Poêles, Stéphane Mouton, one of the last bell-founders in France, supervised the operation. After the melting of 8.5 tonnes of a bronze alloy (eighty percent copper and twenty percent tin), which took about nine hours, a solemn blessing of the moulds preceded the casting of the first three bells. As the priests left the foundry, Stéphane and his team of twelve adjusted their gear – thick gloves, overalls and helmets with long faceguards. They stood ready, waiting for their boss's signal. 'Let's go!' shouted Stéphane as he opened a little door in the foundry's oven. In just a few minutes, the molten metal ran down into the moulds. Movements had to be precise and swift, the seeping gas set alight immediately to prevent an explosion and moulds sealed as soon as the metal settled and ceased moving. Those were tense and dangerous moments. 'Get back, Daniel. Your foot! Get back!' screamed Stéphane to his colleague across the room, fearing his closeness to the molten metal. When the completion of the operation was announced, everyone started applauding. 'It is always special,' said Stéphane, choking with emotion. 'Why? Because it is always different, because it's both magical and solemn, and because the bells are for Notre-Dame. You can imagine: if I am emotional here, casting them in the foundry, how will people feel when they actually hear them ring for the first time in Paris?'[5]

The bell-sculptor Virginie Bassetti conceived their decoration and drew with chalk her first sketches for the bells' crowns and waists on the clay mould. Virginie imagined dancing flames, the fire of faith and passion, girdling them. Saint Augustine's motto '*Via viatores quaerit*' (I am the path that seeks travellers) was to feature on their crowns. She would also draw a few crosses and the Virgin Mary with her infant under the name of each bell.

Their names were carefully chosen. Gabriel bears the name of the archangel who foretold the birth of Jesus to his mother, the Virgin Mary; Anne-Geneviève is named after both the Virgin's mother and the patron saint of Paris; Denis after Paris's first bishop in the third century; Marcel after Saint Marcel, Paris's ninth bishop in the fourth century; Étienne after the early martyr and the ancient cathedral that once stood in place of Notre-Dame; Benoît-Joseph is a tribute to Pope Benedict XVI, Joseph Ratzinger; Maurice is an homage to Bishop Maurice de Sully, who conceived and financed the construction of Notre-Dame; and Jean-Marie is named in memory of the much-loved Cardinal Jean-Marie Lustiger, archbishop of Paris between 1981 and 2005 and a converted Jew. Together, those eight bells weigh 16.6 tonnes. Marie is named after Notre-Dame's first-ever bourdon, cast in 1378. Marie would join Emmanuel, whose name was chosen by King Louis XIV himself, in the south tower.

After the founders removed the moulds, sanded them and pounced them in, the bells finally appeared in their bright, shiny silver robes. It was time to study their sound spectrum; each has a unique voice and is tuned to a specific note. Paul Bergamo of the foundry recorded them for posterity: G sharp Marie and Maurice, A sharp Gabriel and Jean-Marie, Anne-Geneviève and her B, C sharp Denis, D sharp Marcel, F sharp Benoît-Joseph and Étienne and his F – all in tune with each other and with the eldest, bourdon Emmanuel, eagerly awaiting them.

If Emmanuel only chimes on great occasions, such as at midnight on Christmas Day and for exceptional national events, the other nine are in constant use for the five daily religious services (seven on Sundays), not to mention ringing the hours.

*

On Palm Sunday 2013, at 5.30 p.m., the parvis was already packed with a huge crowd that had come to hear the cathedral's new voice: there were many families, many tourists too. On the Left Bank Parisians discussed the best spot from which to hear, their fingers raised to sense the direction of the wind. The little garden of Saint-Julien-le-Pauvre on quai Montebello was crammed with people. Bridges were also soon thronged with bystanders spilling out onto the streets. The advantage of standing on the parvis was that there were giant screens broadcasting images from inside the towers with close-ups of the new bells.

And then it began. At 6.06 p.m., after a few words from Monsignor Jacquin, the yoke of the first pair of bells in the north tower started moving gently, the clappers struck the bells, at first slowly, then more vigorously, as if getting into the mood. Another pair of bells joined in, swinging on the giant screens. Applause was followed by silence; Paris was listening to the harmonious voice of its long-distant past, a pre-revolutionary past. On the streets Parisians looked at Notre-Dame and then at each other, smiling. Some commented on the new melodious sounds with an awed 'Ah!' and excited 'Oh!', while others, clearly musicians, recognized their different tones.

'That's Gabriel ringing now!' a mother said to her child. There were many misty eyes in the crowd too. Stéphane Mouton was right.

There is something profoundly blissful and moving about bells swinging and ringing, something childlike and carefree, both optimistic and nostalgic, a link between past and present. Victor Hugo wrote about Notre-Dame's bells in *Notre-Dame de Paris*: 'There had been peals for every occasion, long morning serenades, which lasted from prime to compline; peals from the belfry for a High Mass, rich scales drawn over the smaller bells for a wedding, for a christening, and mingling in the air like a rich embroidery of all sorts of charming sounds. The old church, all vibrating and sonorous, was in a perpetual joy of bells.'

Hugo also wrote about the elation felt by Quasimodo who, though deaf, lived in sync with the cathedral's bells:

When he had set them to swing, when he felt that cluster of bells moving under his hand, when he saw, for he did not hear it, the palpitating octave ascend and descend that sonorous scale, like a bird hopping from branch to branch; when the demon Music, that demon who shakes a sparkling bundle of strettos, trills and arpeggios, had taken possession of the poor deaf man, he became happy once more, he forgot everything, and, his heart expanding, made his face beam.[6]

The late French medievalist Georges Duby would probably have invoked the serenity which infused the art of France of the twelfth and thirteenth centuries, the Gothic art that 'became the smiling expression of joy',[7] to explain Quasimodo's elation, and indeed our own beaming faces each time we hear Notre-Dame's bells. After all, the Gothic dream was a symphonic one: 'that the coherence of light be used to extract the essential oneness of liturgical celebration; that all officiants be gathered in unison, all gestures harmonize like voices, all voices raised as one voice'.[8]

Of course, the significance of Notre-Dame's bells goes beyond the simple delight of hearing them on a daily basis. They have accompanied French history for the last 850 years, they have provided the soundtrack to our national sorrow and our triumphant joy. As the historian and *résistant* André Chamson put it:

> The echoes of our glory and our losses, of our victories and our disasters, have always resounded under those vaults. We have always tolled the bells for our dead, sounded the tocsin of our anger and the carillon of our joys with the bourdon of its towers. Atheists and believers may share there the same memories, for they are France's memories.[9]

On 8 January 2015, at midday, under icy rain, thousands of Parisians gathered in front of Notre-Dame to hear her bells toll for the dead of *Charlie Hebdo*. Many people were carrying pencils in their hands, to salute the cartoonists assassinated by radical Islamists the day before. What was spectacular and particularly poignant was the sadness expressed by a Catholic cathedral at the death of staunch atheists, most of them anti-clerical with a passion. The satirical magazine had always been scathingly anti-religious, and particularly critical of Catholicism, but magnanimous Notre-Dame never seems to bear grudges. Ten months later, Our Lady would also toll for the 130 victims of the 13 November 2015 attacks, equally for those who believed in heaven and for those who didn't.

*

Bells and the Grand Organ have always played an important role in the life and history of the cathedral. The organist in 1789 almost single-handedly saved Notre-Dame from more destruction at the hands of French revolutionaries after he astutely chose to play only the 'Marseillaise' and revolutionary songs and music.

Since the thirteenth century Notre-Dame has had a choir and been a choir school, today with 165 singers, thirty-five teachers and four organists. This 'immaterial heritage' has somehow been forgotten after the fire of April 2019. Today, while the bells are silenced during the reconstruction, Notre-Dame's choir is in exile and will have to tour the world in order to survive. Happily, it has friends.

Veronika Wand-Danielsson is one of them. The Swedish ambassador in Paris was attending a birthday party in Cairo on the evening of the fire. 'We were devastated – the dinner ended abruptly – we just watched the television in disbelief; many of us, seasoned diplomats, were in tears,' she recalled a few months later. 'The people in the street in Cairo also seemed deeply touched. They can relate to Notre-Dame, they saw it as a European pyramid, as if the Kheops pyramid were to collapse and disappear . . .'[10]

The Swedish embassy in Paris has a special relationship with Notre-Dame. On 13 December, the feast day of Saint Lucy,

Sweden's patron saint, the royal choir of Stockholm joins that of Notre-Dame for a concert in the cathedral. 'We have immediately decided to maintain the tradition and the concert will continue to be performed in other great churches of Paris like Saint-Sulpice, just next to August Strindberg Square.' However, for Veronika Wand-Danielsson it was not enough merely to maintain ties: Sweden needed to help Notre-Dame in some meaningful way. In the fire, Notre-Dame's choir and school lost everything: their instruments, their music sheets and their albs – and, even more importantly, the place where they performed fifty sold-out concerts and 1,000 religious services a year. The Swedish prime minister, Stefan Löfven, and his ambassador in Paris approached Swedish companies such as Ikea, Electrolux and Saab, which together with some others gathered a million Swedish kronor[11] for Notre-Dame's choir. 'And I personally checked that the money was transferred,' says Veronika with a smile.

Her architecture and music have made Notre-Dame 'a work of total art', or *Gesamtkunstwerk*. This is probably why she has inspired so many artists and thinkers, from Claude Monet to Auguste Rodin, Victor Hugo and Marcel Proust, even Sigmund Freud, whose works were conceived as, and built like, cathedrals.

11

2019

The Battle for the Reconstruction of Notre-Dame

'We will rebuild her even more beautiful than before.'

Emmanuel Macron[1]

I t was 2 a.m. when General Jean-Claude Gallet, who was doing yet another inspection of the cathedral, noticed a patch of light on the lectionary on what remained of the altar. From the dust-covered page the word 'hope' leapt out at him, but it was his determination and the resolve and courage of hundreds of fire-fighters willing to risk their lives that kept Notre-Dame standing. Born and raised on the coast of the Vendée in the south-west of France, 'a land of mercenaries', the general is not a believer. To atheists, miracles are coincidences.

Throughout the night, while General Gallet and his men were doing their rounds and keeping the fire under control, thousands of Parisians and tourists, unable to sleep, ebbed and flowed towards Notre-Dame. To keep vigil, to wish her strength and to inspect her injuries. As dawn broke, those holding binoculars could make out colours and animal figures in the south rose window; they looked and looked again, both shocked and relieved. Hadn't the lead seal of each stained-glass panel melted? How could the rose windows have survived such a furnace? Miraculous, surely.

This new day was going to be full of both sorrow and wondrous tidings. The bees of Notre-Dame, living on the roof of the sacristy, were soon spotted going in and out of their hives. This was the news Sybile Moulin, their 33-year-old keeper and a doctor of biology, hadn't dared hope for. She had visited them only ten days earlier; she knew how resilient they were. Still, to survive both water and fire of such magnitude required luck – or the help of Providence. She was overjoyed when she saw aerial pictures showing, next to the devastated roof, three small dots, her three beehives, still in place.[2] When she received a short video shot by the sacristan showing bees happily buzzing around their skeps, she was completely reassured. 'They have a safety mechanism: when they feel the smoke, they gorge on honey and surround their queen to protect her.'

Sybile Moulin and her boss, Nicolas Géant, installed the beehives in April 2013 as part of a movement to revive urban biodiversity and bring back bees to the heart of megalopolises such as Paris. Today, Paris is home to more than 700 beehives. Many are kept atop the roofs of buildings and monuments such as the Opéra, the Musée d'Orsay and the Grand Palais. In fact, French cities are greener than many parts of the countryside: there may be more cars but very little pesticide, fungicide and insecticide, the real killers. The 200,000 bees of Notre-Dame are Brother Adam bees, an especially gentle variety, producing on average 25 kilos of honey a year, which is sold exclusively to the cathedral staff.

What about the Grand Organ? Could it, too, have survived the fire, perched 16 metres above the main portals, in what is known as the 'swallows' nest'? Fat chance, thought Olivier Latry, one of the three cathedral organists, who had just landed in Vienna for a concert. He put down his luggage in his hotel room when he received a text, and then a second with a picture: Notre-Dame's roof on fire. He spent the night prostrate in front of the TV screen. A few weeks earlier he had recorded an album of organ music called *Bach to the Future*, on the cover of which he lies horizontal as if levitating. The last music to have been recorded in Notre-Dame before the fire was a vibrant homage to Baroque Lutheran music. How apt and ecumenical.

From Vienna he thinks about this ogre of an instrument, a Cavaillé-Coll dating back to 1868, some of whose pipes are hundreds of years old. It took him five years to learn how to use it and he always thought it would take a lifetime to tame 'its extraordinary personality'.[3] In 2013 it had been restored and equipped with a new console made of white sycamore and twenty-one new stops (each stop corresponds to the collection of pipes of the same timbre), and every single one of the 7,374 pipes had been cleaned by hand. In fact, the Grand Organ of Notre-Dame has been continually restored and augmented through time, growing organically. Over the centuries almost every great organ-builder worked on it, modernizing it as they went along, adding the best technology of the time and making it an astonishing musical synthesis.

Olivier Latry couldn't come to terms with the idea that just thirty-six hours earlier, on Palm Sunday, he was there, his hands jumping over the five manuals, his feet dancing on the pedals, towering above Notre-Dame's nave. 'It was a beautiful service. Especially the moment when the priest knocked on the cathedral door with his processional cross and demanded to be allowed in.' He let the organ's full volume swell, sending musical colours reverberating around the Gothic building. 'It sounded like Christ was entering the cathedral.'[4]

Luck struck again. The day after the fire the Grand Organ was declared saved, just like the stained-glass rose windows and the beehives. It had suffered only minor damage, having been protected by a slightly sloping stone roof: the fire-fighters' water just ran off it, avoiding the instrument. The thousands of pipes were, it seemed, just terribly dusty and would have to be cleaned again.

*

The fate of the Grand Organ must have particularly preoccupied Philippe Villeneuve when he finally reached the cathedral, having hopped on the last high-speed train to Paris from La Rochelle; he arrived on the parvis at 11 p.m. knowing that the structure had been saved. As a chief architect at Historic Monuments Villeneuve is familiar with every nook and cranny, every corner, secret passage and hidden door of the monument. He still owns two postcards of the cathedral he bought when he was six. As a teenager, while his sister was listening to Pink Floyd, he would lock himself in his room to play records by Pierre Cochereau. 'That night, I died,' Philippe Villeneuve says candidly, before explaining: 'Notre-Dame is constitutive of my being.' His destiny espouses that of a cathedral he was put in charge of in 2013, and the rebuilding of the cathedral will no doubt mirror his own healing.

A few years ago, Villeneuve had alerted the Ministry of Culture to the degraded state of the cathedral. His lengthy rounds of inspection had made him aware that she was greatly suffering, not only from decay but, increasingly, from the effects of pollution, climate change and acid rain. He had noticed the fragility of some flying buttresses, erosion of masonry, loosening of stained-glass panels and fissuring of stones and sculptures. He had drawn up a list of the broken gargoyles replaced by plastic pipes, crumbled balustrades propped up by wooden planks and pinnacles held together by straps. In some parts the limestone even crumbled at the touch of his finger. At the time he assessed the costs of the restoration as at least a hundred million euros. The state, which has owned Notre-Dame since the Law on the Separation of Church and State of 1905, agreed to release sixty million while the Church, being, as it keeps saying, only the beneficiary, looked the other way.

In a country where people traditionally rely on the state for almost everything in life and where private philanthropy still sounds too foreign a concept, brave souls attempted to raise funds in and outside France to contribute to Notre-Dame's restoration works. The Friends of Notre-Dame foundation was created to find patrons, especially in the United States, and after a twelve-month campaign two million euros were raised to help Villeneuve's ten-year restoration plans. The sums didn't amount to the hundred million needed, but the urgency meant that work could at least start, and in summer 2018 a giant metallic mantilla started covering the *flèche*. The spire was indeed first on the list of priorities. Four days before the fire, the sixteen copper statues representing the twelve apostles and four evangelists, 3.4 metres high and weighing 150 kilos, had been removed by a giant crane and transported to Périgueux in the heart of the Dordogne to be restored by the Socra company. One of the statues was different from the others. Saint Thomas, patron saint of architects, famously bore the traits of his creator, Eugène Viollet-le-Duc. He alone among the sixteen holy giants situated at the base of the spire did not look at Paris, spread at their feet. Instead, holding a long architect's ruler, he stared up at the spire, watchful.

The fire changed everything. Coffers would soon be bursting with money for Notre-Dame. It almost took her complete destruction for people's love to materialize. Guilt played an essential role. Her well-being was of course our collective responsibility. In the middle of the night, France's richest families, afflicted too by this vision of hell just like the rest of their compatriots, took generous decisions. Eighty-two-year-old François Pinault, son of a modest timber merchant from Brittany, quickly called his son François-Henri, now head of the family company, the world-class luxury group Kering.[5] Together they decided to pledge a hundred million euros to Notre-Dame's reconstruction from their family fund and not seek the tax breaks normally granted to such donations.[6]

Ten days earlier, François Pinault had travelled to Guernsey to reopen Hauteville, the house where Victor Hugo lived in exile from 1855 to 1870. Having personally financed its restoration, Pinault would have remembered walking through the entrance of the house, where a Corinthian column supports

Victor Hugo's very own tympanum. The writer, who loved interior design, had it made by local craftsmen in March 1858 from oak and brass. It reprised the cover illustration from the first edition of *Notre-Dame de Paris*.[7] Hauteville House, which Hugo designed from floor to ceiling, was thus conceived as his very own Gothic cathedral, with stark contrasts of light between dark vestibules and bright alcoves. To visit Hauteville is to enter Hugo's mind and hear him talk via all the sentences he carved on the oak-panelled walls. Worded in French and Latin, his fiercely progressive republican mottos were interwoven with his ardent Catholic faith. In the kitchen, a statuette of the Virgin holding the infant Jesus has been transformed into an allegory of Liberty with, all around her, the words of Hugo:[8]

> *Le peuple* is small, but will become great
> In your sacred arms, O fecund mother
> O holy liberty with your conquering step
> You hold the child who will carry the world.

Still absorbed in visions of Hugo's den, and no doubt inspired by the writer's words, Pinault must have felt all the more stirred by images of Notre-Dame ablaze. He also remembered how the success of *Notre-Dame de Paris* saved her from dereliction.[9] He thus became the trailblazer of a formidable outpouring of generosity, from rich and poor, in France and elsewhere.

The Pinaults were immediately followed by Bernard Arnault, France's richest man, head of the luxury group LVMH and ever the competitor: he doubled Pinault's pledge and offered 200 million euros towards the rebuilding. So, shortly afterwards, did the Bettencourt family, heir to L'Oréal, while the oil and gas company Total announced it would contribute a hundred million euros. In comparison, the deluge of twenty-, ten- and five-million-euro donations by extremely wealthy individuals such as the Decaux, Bouygues and Ladreit de Lacharrière families in France and the Disneys and Kravises in the US looked almost small, although they too, of course, were momentous acts of generosity. And everyone followed suit according to their wealth. A cascade of donations started falling into the purses of four main foundations: the Fondation de France, the Fondation du Patrimoine, the Centre des Monuments Nationaux and the Fondation Notre-Dame.

The smaller donations were particularly touching. The municipality of Szeged in Hungary voted to send 10,000 euros. It had never forgotten how, after the city suffered devastating flooding in March 1879, Paris sent financial help for its rebuilding. One hundred and forty years later, gratitude was being repaid in kind. The king of Sanwi, a kingdom on the Ivory Coast, pledged to help the cathedral where his ancestor, Prince Aniaba, godson of Louis XIV, had been christened in 1702.

Solidarity works in all kinds of ways. And sometimes, from one building to another. The Palace of Versailles, which was to raise funds for its own restoration works the day after the fire through a charity auction of rare Château Mouton-Rothschild wines in London, decided during the night to give all the proceeds to Notre-Dame. One million dollars. From Versailles to Notre-Dame, with love.

Monsignor Benoist de Sinety, vicar-general of Paris, read the first of the thousands of letters sent to the cathedral. 'It's the smallest donations that move me the most,' he says. Especially the letters from children who, all over the world, insisted their family didn't give them a birthday present but donated instead to the rebuilding of Notre-Dame. Or this French lady who slipped a ten-euro note in an envelope with a few lines: 'My family is not well off but this is for Notre-Dame. The 15 April was my birthday which I spent crying for Our Lady.' Exactly two months after the fire, eighty million euros[10] had been received through small gifts and could be spent immediately, while the big donations needed go through a well-known and lengthy process of conventions between the donor and the state carrying out the reconstruction.

Being France, such lavish generosity from private donors and well-known billionaires infuriated a small but vocal part of public opinion. On 16 April, around 8 a.m., Notre-Dame's embers still warm, the young baker from Chez Isabelle, usually so gentle, with his blond fringe, clear blue eyes and easy smile, was fuming with rage. 'Ready to give hundreds of millions for a cathedral, but what about the people in need?' He was not alone in thinking this way.

The Church of France felt the simmering anger and, for once, was quick to react. 'The rich need guidance with their generosity. They should be encouraged to give to Notre-Dame as well as to people in need. However, in my experience, someone who starts giving keeps on giving and is grateful to be asked to help,'[11] said Monsignor de Sinety, who knows the crucial importance of private donations. He was for eleven years priest of the iconic Left Bank church of Saint-Germain-des-Prés, recently restored to its former glory thanks, in part, to the generosity of American philanthropists. An initiative he came up with in 2017 proved very popular: donors could adopt one of the five thousand golden stars on the blue celestial vault of the choir. Monsignor de Sinety is hoping that the vast amount pledged to Notre-Dame can in time benefit other charitable initiatives and churches, people as well as old stones.

However, the anger from some corners at seeing the lavish generosity of the rich and powerful for 'just a crumbling old church' wasn't going to abate anytime soon. In France, egalitarianism is akin to a religion. Wealth is an object of fascination *and* execration. The Gilets Jaunes movement, a clear expression of the latter, unfailingly criticized the numbers of millions the very privileged were ready to spend as soon as donations were made public. If no Gilets Jaunes could articulate in a cogent way what they found indecent in the outpouring of wealth towards Notre-Dame, others could: for instance Gaël Giraud, a Jesuit priest and an economist.[12] For him, this overflow of money was first of all the sign that it is indeed right and proper to tax the rich heavily, so that the state can redistribute its tax revenues towards the citizens most in need. He also urged the Church to use some of those donations for migrants and the three million children living below the poverty line in France. He invoked the Bible and Luke 22:25, where Christ tells the apostles during the Last Supper that the rich often use their generosity in order to exert power on others: 'And he said unto them, The kings of the Gentiles exercise lordship over them; and they that exercise authority upon them are called benefactors.'

After suspicion emerged that rich contributors were in fact more interested in their donations' tax breaks than in

Notre-Dame, the Pinaults, Arnaults and Bettencourts, knowing their compatriots all too well, announced they wouldn't seek any of the usual and perfectly legal tax rebates that existed for such donations. Their generosity was sincere, and they wanted it to be known.

Gaël Giraud goes further in his analysis: he insists on the fact that Notre-Dame's fire has revealed a profound malaise, both in France and elsewhere in the Western world. 'Our technological society shows how vulnerable it in fact is. We're capable of going to the moon and yet we can't even protect Notre-Dame's 800-year-old roof from fire.' Until the last century nobody had dared to introduce electricity into the cathedral, but now that we have, we cannot bring ourselves to take responsibility for the consequences. 'As for politics,' Giraud says, 'it has been discredited by the omnipotence of financial markets, which we have let rule our world.' The problem is that 'big finance has proved both irrational and inefficient, unable to give any meaning to our lives. When Notre-Dame is in flames, it is our social fabric that is burning.'

The Church has played a major role in Europe: it helped create the state, it built hospitals and schools, it wrote the first codified body of laws, also known as canon law, and provided Europe's first administration. In many ways Notre-Dame embodies this chapter of our history. And the emotion at seeing her burn, mirrors our confusion at witnessing the foundations of our social bond and cultural fabric disintegrate. As long as symbols such as Notre-Dame exist, we can hold on to the hope that our societies haven't completely given in to financialization and have even retained this link with the transcendental that we haven't completely renounced. Giraud concludes: 'We are keenly aware that the disappearance of places like Notre-Dame would lead to a lethal anomy.'[13]

*

Focused on the momentous task ahead and oblivious to the controversies already brewing, National Heritage curator Marie-Hélène Didier, chief architects at Historic Monuments and the many contractors who were present on the site for weeks before the fire – stone-carvers, scaffolding workers, roofers, carpenters, rope-access technicians, climbing riggers – are back at dawn on 16 April to assist Philippe Villeneuve. Among them is Didier Durand, the grandson of an Italian mason, heading the Pierre Noël company and a team of forty-seven stonemasons, splitters, cutters and carvers. The Ministry of Culture calls Durand to say they will immediately send him a new contract: length, amount and cost of work unspecified.

Time is of the essence. There are two main priorities: assessing the immediate needs, and stabilizing and strengthening Notre-Dame.

Accompanied by fire-fighters, Marie-Hélène Didier enters the nave to inspect the state of the famous thirteen 'Mays'. She also urgently needs to attend to the 1,000 art objects left after the rescue the night before, the oldest of which date back to the sixteenth century, as well as the monumental carpets and, last but not least, the famous fourteenth-century *Vierge à l'enfant* (Virgin with infant), also known as 'Notre-Dame de Paris'. She was told that the Virgin had been spotted still standing by the south-west pillar of the transept in what was now a *zone interdite* (no-go area). But in what state?

Will Marie-Hélène find the Virgin who has personified Notre-Dame de Paris as lovely as she had left her, so elegant, with her melancholy, mysterious smile and her child playing with the fold of her coat? Since 1818, the year she was gifted to Notre-Dame, the tilt of her hip has made her stand out among the thirty-seven Virgin Marys represented in the cathedral. 'Pretty and yet so bizarre, with her joyous smile on such melancholic lips!' wrote the French decadent writer Joris-Karl Huysmans in 1898. 'Seen from one side, she smiles at Jesus, almost mockingly [. . .] Seen from another, this smile vanishes. The lips, pursed, may be heralding tears. Perhaps, by achieving opposite feelings in Our Lady, peace and fear, the sculptor meant to express the joy of nativity and the distant pain of the suffering of the cross.'[14]

Marie-Hélène is stunned: every piece of art, every painting, every statue is intact, slightly dusty but not even blackened with soot. The fall of the spire at the crossing of the transept created a flue effect, like a chimney, and sucked out most of the smoke. Remarkably, the rest of the vaults have held, as planned by their medieval creators. Vaults were designed very precisely in order to protect a cathedral from fire. 'Arches, ribs, vaults have admirably played their part,' confirms Philippe Villeneuve.

However, the waterlogged walls and stone mean that all the paintings must be quickly taken down, and nobody knows how the edifice is going to react as the water very slowly evaporates. For two weeks Marie-Hélène Didier hardly sleeps, doesn't read any of the hundreds of daily messages she receives and avoids newspapers. On the rare occasions when she does look at them they are so full of inaccuracies, sterile controversies about donations and laughable designs for the new spire that she prefers to block it all out. She starts relaxing a little after the 200-kilo *Vierge à l'enfant* is put to safety, thanks to an elaborate system of traction pulleys and wheeled scaffolding already used by the Romans.

*

Philippe Villeneuve, too, has very little time for the fantastical, if not plain weird, designs for the new spire which start flooding social media and the pages of every newspaper. Going up and down the cathedral, pacing the nave from east to west, crawling, climbing, jumping, squatting, he wants to be able to get a precise idea of its state. He has forbidden all workers to walk in the nave because the vaults' equilibrium is so precarious; they could collapse at any moment.[15] His eyes scan every stone: if he fails in his immediate assessment of the damage, this could have dramatic consequences. In other words, 'it is war',[16] and it will remain so until Notre-Dame is considered completely stabilized and consolidated.

Villeneuve needs 127 metres by 48 metres of waterproof tarpaulin to cover the vaults. And he needs it now. The weather forecast is clear: it will rain over Paris on Friday, in three days' time. Rope-access technicians are ready, tarpaulin is found. Working round the clock, climbers finish covering the cathedral's roof a few hours before heavy rain and gale-force winds start lashing Paris.

The north gable is of extreme concern for Philippe Villeneuve. A 350-tonne pillar which used to be attached to the timber roof but is now precariously standing without any support threatens to collapse on the gable. If it falls inwards, it will then in all likelihood take the north rose window down with it; if it falls outwards, it will topple the six-storey Haussmann-era building standing opposite on rue du Cloître-Notre-Dame. Didier Durand, the master stonemason, tells Villeneuve that he sees only one way in which he can immediately start securing the north gable: by cutting the 1.8-tonne head off the statue of an archbishop at its top. Fire-fighters hesitate before agreeing to the highly risky manoeuvre and a field hospital is set up in rue du Cloître-Notre-Dame. While Durand goes up the spiral stairs to monitor the operation, a crane lifts one of his workers to a height of 46 metres, hanging in a basket, chainsaw in hand. The slightest wind and things could turn ugly. The operation takes six hours. 'I aged ten years,'[17] confides Durand. Later, 18-metre-long wooden beams arrive from Belgium, the closest place they could be found, to consolidate either side of the gable.

The west gable, linking the two towers, and the chimera gallery tell another story. Twenty-metre-high tongues of fire have licked the stone through the oculus for hours. The stone has turned a beautiful pink, but a few angels have cracked open in the heat. The Angel of the Last Judgment, split in two, has to be removed. Many gargoyles must be strapped from head to toe, while others are wrapped up in fresh plaster and cellophane and taken down to be stored in an improvised lapidarium on the parvis.

The masonry of the south gable has also suffered greatly. The laboratory will tell if elements of it can be reused. 'If the heart is intact, even though they are rubified, and now pink, we will use them again,' says Philippe Villeneuve, who favours 'homeopathic restoration'. In the nave, Villeneuve realizes that two pillars must be bound with copper tape at once as they are highly likely to crumble under pressure – cracks are appearing here and there over their entire length. He also orders that every stained-glass panel be unsealed and stored away.

Up to 150 expert artisans start to work almost day and night to stabilize Notre-Dame, but so much must be done, and on so many fronts at the same time. Six robots, two sweeping, four equipped with pliers, are sent into the nave for ten hours a day to collect the charred debris, every inch of which must be inspected, sorted, numbered and stored for yet further inspection by two separate teams, one comprising forensic experts for the ongoing criminal investigation into the cause of the fire, the other consisting of archaeologists and experts in stone, metal, wood and glass. Philippe Villeneuve has warned his team: 'We will keep every bit of stone and reuse it if we can.'

Because of the way in which Notre-Dame was built, Philippe Villeneuve must consider the different elements of her intricate structural system simultaneously. A Gothic cathedral such as Our Lady doesn't rely on the heavy mass of its walls for support but distributes weight through columns, pillars, external flying buttresses and counter-supports. The spire and the roof, intentionally made heavy with lead, both contributed to the general health of the structure. Their disappearance suddenly endangers Notre-Dame's whole fabric, her whole existence.

It soon becomes clear that each of the twenty-eight flying buttresses (fourteen for the choir and fourteen for the nave) needs to be reinforced with inner semi-circular wooden arches, like an exoskeleton. If vaults fall, it is crucial that walls don't collapse as a result, pushed as they would be by the flying buttresses. Besides, those inner wooden arches will help support the future gigantic umbrella when Notre-Dame reaches her reconstruction stage.

All this, this race to reinforce and stabilize Notre-Dame, is costing a fortune; workers and suppliers need to be paid on time and the usual funds at the Ministry of Culture have dried up quickly. As for the eighty million euros collected from thousands of small donors, they won't last long. On 2 July 2019 Philippe Villeneuve invites François Pinault to witness the fitting of the first supporting wooden arch. 'I took pictures but they are all blurred. I was so afraid, I was shaking,' says Villeneuve a few weeks later. The first 8-tonne wooden arch is lifted up 40 metres by crane and must be fitted like a glove with the help of climbers. On seeing such skill and dedication, François Pinault agrees to release ten million euros immediately, even though no contract has been agreed yet. He understands the urgency and so does Bernard Arnault, who also advances ten million euros towards the mounting costs.

*

Unbeknownst to the team of architects, curators and master masons tending night and day to Notre-Dame's injuries, extravagantly fanciful designs for a new spire were now flooding social networks and newspapers worldwide. With his admirable determination to see Notre-Dame rebuilt 'more beautiful than before' in just 'five years', the French president had unleashed the wildest imaginations. The day after, and only two days after the fire, Prime Minister Édouard Philippe was feeding the general frenzy by launching an international competition for the design of the new spire, calling for it to be 'adapted to the techniques and the challenges of our era'. A general state of hysteria seemed to be *le sentiment du jour.*

For the roof, one French firm proposed a giant greenhouse, while another suggested a forest planted on a terrace where endangered animal species would find refuge. A Swedish architect offered a cross-shaped swimming pool filled with rainwater, another a glass conservatory – all environmentally friendly of course. As for the spire, a debate raged about its material: crystal, glass or titanium; someone said that it should not be rebuilt at all, just replaced by a beam of light. Its shape? It didn't need to be spire-like, many reasoned.

The French designer Matthieu Lehanneur thought that he too would offer his take on it, except that he meant it ironically. He posted on Instagram a picture of the cathedral with a gleaming 100-metre flame made of carbon fibre and covered in gold leaf. His provocation was taken very seriously and took social media by storm. Even the renowned architect Norman Foster thought no better than to enter the fray, and declared: 'The new spire should be contemporary and very spiritual.' A marvel of vagueness.

Months later, it is easier to consider this outburst of wild designs erupting days after the tragedy as a cathartic response to it. So too must be construed President Macron's determination to rebuild her 'more beautiful than before' in just five years. No doubt the shock of the fire and of having nearly witnessed her collapse prompted him and the whole government to speak in those terms. Psychoanalysts would call it release, a way of letting off the angst that shook us all to the core, the intensely distressing thoughts we bore for a few hours, fearing the worst, powerless as we were in the face of the flames that were ravaging her.

However, such whimsical designs for a new contemporary spire and roof again divided French opinion in the never-ending battle between *les modernes* and *les anciens*. The conservative daily newspaper *Le Figaro* started publishing polls to show that a majority of French people (fifty-five percent) wanted the roof and spire to be rebuilt as before, while an even more crushing majority (seventy-two percent) rejected the Notre-Dame Emergency Act proposed by the government in order to bypass the usual procedures for National Heritage restorations.[18]

*

A public body had to be created to supervise 'the building site of the century', as the French media were now calling it, and President Macron had to choose the right person to run it. He also needed parliament to pass the emergency bill. Notre-Dame could not wait.

First things first: the man or woman to lead the reconstruction. To oversee all the public services which were going to operate hand in hand on the site and the hundreds of technicians, experts, artisans and companies involved in this momentous and historical operation, the French president wanted a leader with natural and moral authority, a scholar with the required historical, religious and artistic knowledge and a fervent Catholic. The five-star general Jean-Louis Georgelin, formerly the French army's chief of staff and recently retired, fitted the bill perfectly. A small office at the Élysée Palace, not far from that of the president, was made available and General Georgelin readily endorsed his new title of 'special representative of the French president'. The Ministry of Culture, feeling sidelined, was not amused. However, President Macron, as ever the doer and with a touch of Bonaparte about him, had a hunch that a military spirit might be just what was needed right here, right now, for Notre-Dame's sake. After all, he had seen the military rigour, valour and bravery of the Paris fire-fighters. In fact, at least in spirit, President Macron was resorting to the alliance of the army and the state to save a symbol of the nation. A historically apt choice.

Passing the Notre-Dame Emergency Act took three months. Both chambers, the National Assembly and the Senate, revised and amended the original text. They, probably wisely, made it less 'exceptional' and reaffirmed the need to follow some well-established procedures, including respecting the knowledge and recommendations of chief architects at Historic Monuments and National Heritage curators. A good way, perhaps, to prevent a planted forest with wild animals from ever replacing Notre-Dame's former roof. However, parliament did agree on the creation of a new public body led by General Georgelin, in which both the Church and the chief architects would have their say.

Of course, Notre-Dame's reconstruction goes far beyond architectural considerations. It presents a formidable opportunity for France to ask itself challenging questions. Big traumas always lead to fundamental questioning and offer renewed opportunities. Jacques Moulin, one of the chief architects at Historic Monuments and in charge of the Gothic cathedrals of Saint-Denis and Meaux, would like to see a complete rethink about how monuments of such historical significance must be protected. Fire alarms are not enough. In his eyes, National Heritage must agree, for instance, to equip those buildings with fire-protection systems. 'There remain a dozen other cathedrals in France with medieval timber roofs, some even older than Notre-Dame. We can't afford to lose another. We must draw the right conclusions in order to prevent such fires from recurring in the future.'[19] Fire protection already exists in warehouses, ranging from nozzle-line water-sprinklers and mist-spraying to saturation humidity to oxygen-depletion systems – a large palette of fire-protection methods to choose from which, somehow, never made it past the Natural Heritage controllers. 'We must of course adapt those invasive systems to historic monuments, but it must be done,' says Moulin. Fire-fighters cannot always be relied upon to risk their lives.

The chief architect also raises a question the Church has always disdainfully dismissed each time it has been brought up: whether to charge an entrance fee to Notre-Dame and other cathedrals of architectural and historical importance, the revenues from which could contribute to the place's upkeep. The Church in France has always rejected the idea, on the noble principle that the house of God should be accessible to all, one which other churches in Europe have adhered to in spirit but not in practice. In Italy, for instance, tourists must pay an entrance fee of a few euros to visit churches of architectural and artistic importance, while worshippers or believers attending religious services are exempted. To this the French Church will invariably reply that it doesn't own any of its churches, at least those built before the 1905 Law on the Separation of Church and State, and that it is therefore the duty of the state to pay for all upkeep, repairs and restoration works.

The 1905 law has infantilized the Church. Preferring not to feel responsible for buildings it does not own any more, thinking of itself solely as their beneficiary, the French Church has behaved loftily and relied on the state for all bricks-and-mortar issues while claiming to focus on people's souls instead. For Jacques Moulin, 'the Church's behaviour has proved a strategic weakness'.[20] Had the French clergy asked Notre-Dame's fourteen million tourists a year to pay a couple of euros for their visit, it would have been able to use those funds for her upkeep. After all, a tenant has duties too.

Will fresh ideas and a newfound maturity come from a younger generation of prelates? Father Gilles Drouin, the priest whom the archbishop of Paris has appointed to supervise the 'liturgy and planning at Notre-Dame de Paris', is certainly open to the discussion. With a PhD in architecture and liturgy in eighteenth-century France, Father Drouin sounds like the right man for the task of reinventing Paris's cathedral when it reopens for worship – everyone's priority, it seems, from General Georgelin to Philippe Villeneuve.

'The Church is going through one of its worst crises. The question, with Notre-Dame but also in general, is: what kind of church experience do we want to give believers today?'[21] declares Father Drouin. For the first time in its 850 years, Notre-Dame's doors are closed; and even if they reopen as soon as the edifice is considered secure, partly roofless but safe, it will still take a couple of years for its methods of visitor access to be rethought. Father Drouin is welcoming this momentous challenge. And the opportunity to confront, at last, and resolve problems which have blighted the reputation of Notre-Dame for decades: endless queues of tourists on the parvis blocking Parisians' passage, inept and time-consuming security checks at the gates, the unattractiveness of cheap souvenir shops inside the cathedral – the list of such unpleasant practicalities is long. What is needed is a complete overhaul, and the possibilities are plentiful.

Why not, for instance, utilize the vacant car park underneath the parvis to organize an access point to the cathedral for tourists, with shops and facilities? Some of this space could be used for the archaeological crypt, which needs a complete review. Why not create a museum in the partly unoccupied Hôtel-Dieu, the former hospital at the heart of Paris standing right across the parvis – as in Milan, where the museum of the Duomo, situated a few steps away from the cathedral, offers an opportunity to understand and learn about its history? So many of Notre-Dame's works of art from across the centuries have been scattered around France in different museums for lack of a dedicated space in Paris, for which many historians, including Adrien Goetz, have been campaigning for years.

Father Drouin is thinking too about the poor of a rich city like Paris and of the changing sociology of city centres. 'Such places of worship must not be so patrimonialised that they become petrified.' Parisians must be able to pop in and out of Notre-Dame the way they do in other churches, and poor people be provided with hot meals just like in other areas of Paris, at the church of Saint-Eustache for instance. Since 1984, from the first day of December to the last day of March, this gem of sixteenth-century architecture has offered, every evening at 7.30, a bowl of hot soup to anyone coming to its steps, no questions asked.

Chief architects at Historic Monuments share similar concerns. They seldom think about old stones in isolation, as if separate from their environment and the people who inhabit them and make them live. Pierre-Antoine Gatier, who still feels too raw about Notre-Dame to be able to talk about her, points to another Notre-Dame he is currently restoring: Notre-Dame-des-Sans-Logis-et-de-Tout-le-Monde, in other words Our Lady of the Homeless and of Everyone. Built in 1957 in the middle of a suburban Parisian slum, this Our Lady was listed as a historic monument in 2016. Refugees and newly arrived immigrants from all parts of the world lived in the slum, where the priest Joseph Wresinski had just been sent.[22] Convinced that beauty was an absolute necessity for this population living in misery, he had an ogival, igloo-shaped church erected, as a tribute to medieval Christian architecture, but this time constructed with fibre cement and recycled materials from waste and scrap. The floor was made of pebbles and the stained-glass windows crafted specially by the abstract expressionist French painter Jean Bazaine.

A few days after the fire, hundreds of Christians were massacred in a church in Sri Lanka during Easter Sunday Mass but the news didn't make it to the front page in the same way Notre-Dame did. This troubled many people, including architects like Gatier, whose passion for architecture and humanity knows no hierarchy.

*

When asked whether he is a believer, Philippe Villeneuve answers 'Joker'.[23] In France it is easier to speak about sex than religion. Religion, as in spirituality, is a deeply personal experience, confined to one's own strict intimacy. In many families, children will never know whether their parents believe or not. It is generally accepted that religion should never be allowed to enter the polity and the life of the city. The separation between state and Church in 1905 was a defining moment for the young republic, an act of emancipation from a power which had ruled over and stifled French society for centuries. It was by taming the Church that the modern republic was founded. Such separation is considered as one of the conditions for a happy cohabitation between atheists and believers, and between ethnically diverse people. The resurgence of religious fundamentalism of all of kinds, Catholic, Muslim and Jewish, for example, has recently tested French secular mettle. In the last thirty years various communities, often manipulated by a fanatical minority, have demanded to be treated differently and to enjoy exceptions from the general rule because of their religion. Torn between guaranteeing social harmony and sticking to the national ethos, the French republic has often found itself bending over backwards, an uncomfortable position.

Notre-Dame's fire has also, but in other ways, tested French resolve. The tragedy revealed that a staunchly secular country had its roots firmly grounded in history, a history that was Christian. Nothing to deplore or to celebrate, a simple fact. This felt like a shock to many French citizens, whose Catholic upbringing or loose notions had been securely buried under a thick layer of secularism and agnosticism. Notre-Dame, a place where the sacred met the secular, reminded us all of where we came from in an unexpected and powerful way.

In France, if someone replies 'Joker' when asked whether they are a believer, it usually means that they do believe in some transcendence and that the answer to this question is a personal and complex one they do not wish to share with a stranger. After uttering the word, Philippe Villeneuve talked of Notre-Dame's beauty as a transcendental experience. To the same question Olivier Latry replied: 'An artist, a musician, is always linked to something higher than themselves. Call it God, if you will. A musician is a link between two dimensions, a human one and another. Playing at the Grand Organ, I often wondered if I was indeed the one making this music. There has to be something else, something other.'[24]

Afterword

Since that fateful night of 15 April 2019, Notre-Dame de Paris has been tended with quiet urgency and profound dedication. There have been many hurdles to leap, from the summer closure of the site due to lead decontamination of the whole Île de la Cité, to lingering fears that Our Lady might still collapse at any time while the structure was being stabilised.

On 1 December 2019, a public body, with five-star general Jean-Louis Georgelin at its head, received the baton from the Paris Prefecture, which had dealt with the cathedral's state of emergency till then. Today General Georgelin oversees the 'building site of the century', as French media have called it, and the international competition for a new spire launched the day after the fire by the French prime minister now seems a distant memory, buried in the drawer of 'good intentions but bad ideas'. The latest thinking is to ask the French people to vote on Notre-Dame's future spire. Philippe Villeneuve, the architect in charge, has already warned he won't be the man to erect a contemporary design. To which General Georgelin responded in military style: 'I have told him many times, and will tell him again if necessary:

he should just shut the fuck up. Only then will we be able to proceed serenely and be able to make the best choice for Notre-Dame, for Paris, for the world.'

Both men are passionate about Notre-Dame, there is no doubt about that, they just express it in their own peculiar and rather Gallic ways. No doubt too that in the years of the reconstruction, there will be more skirmishes and public fallings-out, controversies about private donations and, more importantly, the way the monument should be restored.

General Georgelin and his board of thirteen people, representatives of the state, the Department of Historic Monuments, the Church and the Paris municipality, alongside three committees of scientists, auditors and donors, will report to the French president. Later, hopefully, all being well, the people of France will also have their say.

Notre-Dame de Paris, unlike almost all other cathedrals of her era, does not strike viewers with her flamboyant ornamentation, nor with the prodigal details for which other such monuments are renowned. It is, on the contrary, the simplicity of her shape, the austere majesty of her lines and the overall sense of unity she conveys that stop people in their tracks. As François Théodore de Jolimont wrote in 1823:

> The first feeling one has in front of her is not astonishment, nor is it the kind of excitement and raw emotion one experiences when confronted by an extraordinary implausible edifice. Notre-Dame refuses to flatter the onlooker's imagination. We contemplate her with calm, measure the grandeur of her proportions and enjoy the harmony of it all: our mind approves, and soon it admires.[1]

Awe rather than thrill. The French will probably want to continue feeling awed by her. For she is not just any People's Palace. Notre-Dame is the beating heart of Paris. For more than 850 years, the echo of France's glory and misery, of France's victories and disasters, has resounded under those vaults. For more than 850 years, the French people have tolled for their deaths, sounded the tocsin and chimed their joy with the bells and bourdons of her towers. Atheists and believers can find here the same memories, for they are France's memories. Notre-Dame belongs to every French citizen and every one of them will want to have a say in her future.

There is one moment in particular that many Parisians are looking forward to; it is one that architect Philippe Villeneuve often dreams about. When the spire collapsed on 15 April, the copper rooster perched at its tip fell 96 metres to the ground. Instead of disintegrating like the rest of the spire, made of wood and lead, it just whirled in the air like an incandescent ball and remained in one piece. At dawn, Villeneuve found the battered rooster lying in the gutter of rue du Cloître Notre-Dame. Inside, the relics of Paris's patron saint Genevieve were intact. He understood then that his work of nursing Notre-Dame back to her former glory would only feel complete when he placed the rooster back on the new spire of Notre-Dame. Paris awaits.

Bibliography

BOOKS AND JOURNAL ARTICLES

Auzas, Pierre-Marie, *Les Grandes heures de Notre-Dame de Paris* (Paris: Tel, 1951)

Bazoches, Canon Guillaume de, *Éloge de Paris* (c. 1175)

Bercé, Françoise, (ed.), *La Correspondance Mérimée – Viollet-le-Duc* (Paris: CTHS, 2001)

Bercé, Françoise, *Viollet-le-Duc* (Paris: Patrimoine, 2013)

Boulart, Jean-François *Mémoires militaires du général Baron Boulart sur les guerres de la République et de l'Empire* (Paris: Librairie illustrée, no date)

Bove, Boris and Claude Gauvard (eds.), *Le Paris du Moyen Âge* (Paris: Belin, 2014)

Brassaï, *Conversations avec Picasso* (Paris: Gallimard, 1964)

Cazaux, Yves, *Journal secret de la libération* (Paris: Albin Michel, 1975)

Chapuy and F. T. de Jolimont, *Vues pittoresques de la cathédrale de Paris et détails remarquables de ce monument* (Paris: Leblanc, 1823)

Christiansen, Rupert, *City of Light: The Reinvention of Paris* (London: Head of Zeus, 2018)

Constant, *Mémoires intimes de Napoléon Ier* (Paris: Société des publications littéraires illustrées, 1909)

Correspondance de Napoléon Ier publiée par ordre de l'empereur Napoléon III, 32 vols (Paris, 1858–69)

Delpech, David, *La France de 1799 à 1848: entre tentations despotiques et aspirations libérales* (Paris: Armand Colin, 2014)

Didier, Alexandre, 'Les Origines de la municipalité parisienne', *Mémoires de la Société de l'histoire de Paris et de l'Île de France*, 49, 1927

Dubu, M. *Histoire, description et annales de la basilique de Notre-Dame de Paris* (Paris: Ambroise Bray, 1854)

Duby, Georges, *The Age of the Cathedrals: Art and Society 980–1420*, tr. Eleanor Levieux and Barbara Thompson (London: Croom Helm, 1981)

Erlande-Brandenburg, Alain, *Notre-Dame de Paris* (Paris: Nathan, 1991)

Erlande-Brandenburg, Alain, *Le Roi est mort: étude sur les funérailles, les sépultures et les tombeaux des rois de France jusqu'à la fin du treizième siècle* (Geneva: Droz, 1975)

Gaulle, Charles de, *Mémoires de guerre II: l'unité 1942–1944* (Paris: Plon, 1956)

Glass, Charles, *Americans in Paris: Life and Death under Nazi Occupation 1940–1944* (London: HarperPress, 2009)

Goetz, Adrien *Notre-Dame de l'Humanité* (Paris: Grasset, 2019)

Hugo, Victor, *Notre-Dame de Paris*, tr. Alban Krailsheimer (Oxford: Oxford University Press, 1993)

Huysmans, Joris-Karl, *La Cathédrale* (Paris: Tresse & Stock, 1898)

Jordan, David P., *Transforming Paris: The Life and Labors of Baron Haussmann* (New York: Free Press, 1995)

Kennan, George F., *Sketches from a Life* (New York: Pantheon, 1989)

Kraus, Henry, *L'Argent des cathédrales*, tr. Laurent Medzadourian and Dominique Barrios-Delgado (Paris: Cerf, 2012)

Laveissière, Sylvain, *'Le Sacre de Napoléon' peint par David* (Paris: Louvre, 2004)

L'Estoile, Pierre de, *Journal pour le règne de Henri IV, vol. I: 1589–1600* (Paris: Gallimard, 1948)

Mortet, Victor, *Maurice de Sully, évêque de Paris 1160–1196: étude sur l'administration épiscopale pendant la seconde moitié du XIIe siècle* (Paris: 1890)

Nora, Pierre (ed.), *Les Lieux de Mémoire*, 3 vols (Paris: Gallimard, 1997)

Notre-Dame de Paris 1163–1963: exposition du huitième centenaire organisée par la direction des Archives de France à la Sainte Chapelle, juin–octobre 1963. (Paris: Direction des Archives de France, 1963).

Perrot, Alain-Charles, (ed.), *Les Architectes en chef des monuments historiques 1893–1993, centenaire du concours des ACMH* (Paris: HM, 1994)

Pillorget, René, *Paris sous les premiers Bourbons 1594–1661* (Paris: Hachette, 1988)

Prudhomme, Louis-Marie, *Révolution de Paris* (Paris: Imprimerie des Révolutions, 1792), vol. VII

Roberts, Andrew, *Napoleon: A Life* (London: Penguin, 2014)

Robson, C.A., *Maurice de Sully and the Medieval Vernacular Homily* (Oxford: Basil Blackwell, 1952)

Ségur, Louis-Philippe de, *Extrait du cérémonial relatif au couronnement de Leurs Majestés impériales* (Paris: Imprimerie impériale, Frimaire An XIII (1804))

Spitzer, Sébastien, *Dans les flammes de Notre-Dame* (Paris: Albin Michel, 2019)

Tesson, Sylvain, *Notre-Dame de Paris: Ô reine de douleur* (Paris: Équateurs, 2019)

Viollet-le-Duc, Eugène, *Dictionnaire raisonné de l'architecture française du XIe au XVIe siècle*, 10 vols (Paris: A. Morel, 1854–68)

Viollet-le-Duc, Eugène, 'Du style gothique au XIXe siècle', *Annales archéologiques*, 4, 1846

Viollet-le-Duc, Eugène, *Entretiens sur l'architecture*, 2 vols (Paris: Librairies éditeurs, 1863–72)

WEBSITES (AS AT NOVEMBER 2019)

https://allo18-lemag.fr/notre-dame-dans-la-peau-du-dessinateur-operationnel/

http://www.compagnie-acmh.fr

https://www.defense.gouv.fr/fre/actualites/articles/le-saviez-vous-la-planche-des-pompiers-de-paris

https://www.elysee.fr/emmanuel-macron/2019/04/15/incendie-cathedrale-notre-dame-de-paris

https://www.europe1.fr/societe/il-est-entre-dans-notre-dame-pendant-lincendie-des-morceaux-de-bois-incandescents-tombaient-un-peu-partout-3893436

https://www.francetvinfo.fr/culture/musique/classique/quot-bach-to-the-futurequot-l-039-organiste-olivier-latry-offre-bach-a-notre-dame-de-paris_3293749.html

https://www.francetvinfo.fr/culture/patrimoine/incendie-de-notre-dame-de-paris/seulement-9-des-promesses-de-dons-pour-notre-dame-de-paris-ont-ete-versees_3488763.html

https://www.ina.fr/audio/PHD86069770

https://www.ina.fr/audio/PHD89000578

https://www.ina.fr/video/I00012416/charles-de-gaulle-video.html

https://www.napoleon-empire.net/chronologie/chronologie-1802.php

https://www.notredamedeparis.fr

https://www.pompiersparis.fr/fr/presentation/historique

NEWSPAPER AND MAGAZINE ARTICLES

Beaux Arts, hors série: Notre-Dame de Paris, telle qu'on ne la verra plus!, 23 April 2019

Bommelaer, Claire, 'Les Français opposés à une loi d'exception', *Le Figaro*, 9 May 2019

Ducros, Christine, 'Didier Durand, l'artisan devenu sauveur de Notre-Dame', *Le Figaro*, 24 July 2019

Editorial, *Combat*, 25 August 1944

Hurst, Andrew, '"Miracle" as fireman saves Turin shroud', *Independent*, 13 April 1997

Marshall, Alex, 'Notre-Dame musicians rejoice that the cathedral's organ was spared', *New York Times*, 24 April 2019

Remy, Vincent, 'Notre puissance technique nous rend très vulnérables', *Télérama*, 24 April 2019

Sartre, Jean-Paul, recollection, *Combat*, 2 September 1944

RADIO BROADCASTS

Racines et des Ailes: les 850 ans de Notre-Dame, France 3, March 2013

Notes

All translations from the French are by Agnès Poirier unless otherwise stated.

PROLOGUE

1. Parvis: a court or portico in front of a building. According to the *OED*: Late Middle English from Old French, based on late Latin *paradisus* ('paradise').
2. Brassaï, *Conversations avec Picasso* (Paris: Gallimard, 1964), p. 232.

1. 15 APRIL 2019 – THE NIGHT OF THE FIRE

1. According to Canon Guillaume de Bazoches in *Eloge de Paris*, written around 1175.
2. https://www.notredamedeparis.fr.
3. Monsignor Benoist de Sinety, interview with the author, 11 July 2019.
4. Marie-Hélène Didier, interview with the author, 23 July 2019.
5. http://www.compagnie-acmh.fr.
6. Alain-Charles Perrot (ed.), *Les Architectes en chef des monuments historiques 1893–1993, centenaire du concours des ACMH:* (Paris: HM, 1994).

7. Pierre Cochereau was Notre-Dame's leading organist between 1955 and 1984. He is considered the twentieth century's best organist. Today three organists share the position: Olivier Latry, Vincent Dubois and Philippe Lefebvre.

8. 'La cathédrale en chiffres', Notre-Dame de Paris website, https://www.notredamedeparis.fr/la-cathedrale/les-informations-insolites/la-cathedrale-en-chiffres (accessed 18 November 2019).

9. Philippe Villeneuve, interview with the author, 24 July 2019.

10. General Jean-Claude Gallet, interview with the author, 22 July 2019.

11. 'Historique', Brigade de Sapeurs-Pompiers de Paris website, https:/ /www.pompiersparis.fr/fr/presentation/historique (accessed 18 November 2019).

12. Women account for three percent of the Paris fire brigade.

13. Aude Borel, 'Le saviez-vous? La planche des pompiers de Paris', Ministère des Armées website, 27 July 2016, https://www.defense.gouv.fr/fre/actualites/articles/le-saviez-vous-la-planche-des-pompiers-de-paris (as at August 2019).

14. Adrien Goetz, *Notre-Dame de l'Humanité* (Paris: Grasset, 2019), p. 8.

15. Ibid., p. 9.

16. Ibid., p. 10.

17. Sébastien Spitzer, *Dans les flammes de Notre-Dame* (Paris: Albin Michel, 2019), p. 63.

18. Brigade de Recherche et d'Intervention.

19. 135,000 *livres tournois*, or half the royal wealth.

20. Laurent Prades, interview with the French radio station Europe 1, 17 April 2019. Interview available at https://www.europe1.fr/societe/il-est-entre-dans-notre-dame-pendant-lincendie-des-

morceaux-de-bois-incandescents-tombaient-un-peu-partout-3893436 (accessed 18 November 2019).

21. Spitzer, *Dans les flammes de Notre-Dame*, p. 151.

22. '"All appeared to be lost. Pieces of the Guarini chapel were crashing down and there was a serious danger that it would bury everything – the casket, the altar and all of us," Trematore later explained. So he went in.' Andrew Hurst, '"Miracle" as fireman saves Turin shroud', *Independent*, 13 April 1997.

23. Spitzer, *Dans les flammes de Notre-Dame*, p. 140.

24. As narrated by Laurent Clergeau in the Paris fire brigade's online magazine, *Allo Dix-huit*, https://allo18-lemag.fr/notre-dame-dans-la-peau-du-dessinateur-operationnel/ (accessed 19 November 2019).

25. General Jean-Claude Gallet, interview with the author, 22 July 2019.

26. Ibid.

27. Spitzer, *Dans les flammes de Notre-Dame*, p. 132.

28. Ibid., p. 133.

29. General Jean-Claude Gallet, interview with the author, 22 July 2019.

30. Goetz, *Notre-Dame de l'Humanité*, p. 10.

31. 'Cette cathédrale Notre-Dame, nous la rebâtirons', Élysée website, 15 April 2019, https://www.elysee.fr/emmanuel-macron/2019/04/15/incendie-cathedrale-notre-dame-de-paris (accessed 19 November 2019).

32. Goetz, *Notre-Dame de l'Humanité*, p. 12.

33. Marie-Hélène Didier, interview with the author, 23 July 2019.

34. General Jean-Claude Gallet, interview with the author, 22 July 2019.

2. 1163 – THE FIRST STONE

1. '*Si ce monument est un jour achevé, aucun autre ne pourra lui être comparé.*' Robert de Thorigny was a Norman monk, counsel to Henry II of England and the abbot of Mont-Saint-Michel in Normandy between 1154 and 1186.

2. Henry Kraus, *L'Argent des cathédrales*, tr. Laurent Medzadourian and Dominique Barrios-Delgado (Paris: Cerf, 2012), p. 25.

3. Boris Bove and Claude Gauvard (eds), *Le Paris du Moyen Âge* (Paris: Belin, 2014), p. 7.

4. Roughly today's 1st, 4th and 5th arrondissements.

5. Only officially in 1312, according to Kraus in *L'Argent des cathédrales*, p. 25.

6. Bove and Gauvard, *Le Paris du Moyen Âge*, p. 24.

7. Ibid., p. 26.

8. Alexandre Didier, 'Les Origines de la municipalité parisienne', *Mémoires de la Société de l'histoire de Paris et de l'Île de France*, 49, 1927, p. 266.

9. Kraus, *L'Argent des cathédrales*, p. 27.

10. Georges Duby, *The Age of the Cathedrals: Art and Society 980–1420*, tr. Eleanor Levieux and Barbara Thompson (London: Croom Helm, 1981), p. 112.

11. Ibid., p. 93.

12. Ibid., p. 112.

13. Pierre-Marie Auzas, *Les Grandes Heures de Notre-Dame de Paris: huit siècles d'histoire dans la plus célèbre cathédrale de France* (Paris: Tel, 1951), p. 15.

14. Kraus, *L'Argent des cathédrales*, p. 10.

15. Ibid., p. 37, quoting Victor Mortet, *Maurice de Sully, évêque de Paris 1160–1196: étude sur l'administration épiscopale pendant la seconde moitié du XIIe siècle* (Paris: 1890).

16. Alain Erlande-Brandenburg, *Notre-Dame de Paris* (Paris: Nathan, 1991), p. 50.

17. Obituarium no. 252, quoted in Kraus, *L'Argent des cathédrales*, p. 36.

18. Obituarium no. 214, quoted ibid., p. 36.

19. Ibid., p. 37.

20. Ibid., p. 31.

21. Ibid., p. 43.

22. See C.A. Robson, *Maurice de Sully and the Medieval Vernacular Homily* (Oxford: Basil Blackwell, 1952), pp. 110–13, quoted in Kraus, *L'Argent des cathédrales*, p. 34.

23. Kraus, *L'Argent des cathédrales*, p. 42.

24. Duby, *The Age of the Cathedrals*, p. 94.

25. Kraus, *L'Argent des cathédrales*, p. 39.

26. Duby, *The Age of the Cathedrals*, p. 95.

27. Ibid., p. 155.

28. Pierre Nora (ed.), *Les Lieux de mémoire* (Paris: Gallimard, 1997), vol. III, p. 4185.

29. It is now at the British Museum. Alain Erlande-Brandenburg, *Le Roi est mort: étude sur les funérailles, les sépultures et les tombeaux des rois de France jusqu'à la fin du treizième siècle* (Geneva: Droz, 1975), p. 42.

30. Sylvain Tesson, *Notre-Dame de Paris: Ô reine de douleur* (Paris: Équateurs, 2019), p. 39.

31. Erlande-Brandenburg, *Notre-Dame de Paris*, p. 65.

32. Ibid., p. 50.

33. The baptistery is mentioned in the sixth-century *Vie de Sainte-Geneviève*: Saint Genevieve is reported to have sought shelter in the baptistery in 451 when the town was under attack from Attila.

34. Erlande-Brandenburg, *Notre-Dame de Paris*, p. 54.

35. Ibid., p. 43.

36. Ibid., p. 46.

37. Ibid., p. 46.

38. Ibid., p. 54.

39. Ibid., p. 78.

40. Ibid., p. 78.

41. Ibid., p. 80.

42. Duby, *The Age of the Cathedrals*, p. 147.

43. Nora, *Lieux de mémoire*, vol. III, p. 4185.

44. Alain Erlande-Brandenburg, 'Une tête de prélat provenant du portail du Couronnement de la Vierge à NDP', *Revue du Louvre et des musées de France*, 1986, pp. 186–91.

45. Chapuy and F.T. de Jolimont, *Vues pittoresques de la cathédrale de Paris et détails remarquables de ce monument* (Paris: Leblanc, 1823), p. 5.

46. Duby, *The Age of the Cathedrals*, p. 111.

3. 1594 AND 1638 – THE BOURBONS

1. Wrongly attributed to Henri IV, the saying is first mentioned in 1622 in the satirical *Les Caquets de l'accouchée* and put in the mouth of the Duke of Sully. Nonetheless, the expression, still used today, means that Paris (i.e. power) is well worth the sacrifice of attending a Mass (and by extension a conversion to Catholicism).

2. René Pillorget, *Paris sous les premiers Bourbons 1594–1661* (Paris: Hachette, 1988), p. 12.

3. Pierre de L'Estoile's diary of the time provides an invaluable source on the events described in this chapter. Pierre de L'Estoile, *Journal pour le règne de Henri IV, vol. I: 1589–1600* (Paris: Gallimard, 1948), pp. 375–6.

4. Pierre Nora (ed.), *Lieux de mémoire* (Paris: Gallimard, 1997), vol. III, p. 4190.

5. M. Dubu, *Histoire, description et annales de la basilique de Notre-Dame de Paris* (Paris: Ambroise Bray, 1854), p. 42.

4. 1789 – REASON, SUPREME BEING AND WINE

1. Pierre Nora (ed.), *Lieux de mémoire* (Paris: Gallimard, 1997), vol. III, p. 4197.

2. Ibid., vol. III, pp. 4195–6.

3. Louis-Marie Prudhomme, *Révolution de Paris* (Paris: Imprimerie des Révolutions, 1792), vol. VII, p. 487.

4. M. Dubu, *Histoire, description et annales de la basilique de Notre-Dame de Paris* (Paris: Ambroise Bray, 1854), p. 286.

5. Pierre-Marie Auzas, *Les Grandes Heures de Notre-Dame de Paris: huit siècles d'histoire dans la plus célèbre cathédrale de France* (Paris: Tel, 1951), p. 30.

6. Dubu, *Histoire, description et annales de la basilique de Notre-Dame de Paris*, p. 287.

7. Auzas, *Les Grandes Heures de Notre-Dame de Paris*, p. 30.

5. 1804 – THE CORONATION OF NAPOLEON

1. M. Dubu, *Histoire, description et annales de la basilique de Notre-Dame de Paris* (Paris: Ambroise Bray, 1854), p. 292.

2. A movement (1682) of French Roman Catholic clergy that favoured limiting papal control and introducing greater autonomy.

3. Pierre-Marie Auzas, *Les Grandes Heures de Notre-Dame de Paris: huit siècles d'histoire dans la plus célèbre cathédrale de France* (Paris: Tel, 1951), p. 31.

4. Ibid., p. 30.

5. Ibid., p. 31.

6. Dubu, *Histoire, description et annales de la basilique de Notre-Dame de Paris*, p. 293.

7. 'Napoléon & empire: 1802. La paix et le consulat à vie', https://www.napoleon-empire.net/chronologie/chronologie-1802.php (accessed 20 November 2019).

8. Andrew Roberts, *Napoleon: A Life* (New York: Viking, 2014), p. 329.

9. Ibid., p. 331.

10. The final result was 3,572,329 in favour, 2,579 against. Ibid., p. 348.

11. Napoleon, letter to Pius VII, 15 September 1804, in *Correspondance de Napoléon Ier publiée par ordre de l'empereur Napoléon III* (Paris, 1858–69), vol. IX, p. 525.

12. Napoleon, letter to Cambacérès, 21 September 1804, ibid., vol. IX, p. 675.

13. Sylvain Laveissière, '*Le Sacre de Napoléon*' peint par David (Paris: Louvre, 2004), p. 32.

14. Dubu, *Histoire, description et annales de la basilique de Notre-Dame de Paris*, p. 296.

15. Auzas, *Les Grandes Heures de Notre-Dame de Paris*, p. 31.

16. Laveissière, '*Le Sacre de Napoléon*' peint par David, p. 30.

17. Ibid., p. 31.

18. According to Napoleon's manservant, Constant, who wrote about it in his memoirs: *Mémoires intimes de Napoléon Ier* (Paris: Société des publications littéraires illustrées, 1909), p. 242.

19. Laveissière, '*Le Sacre de Napoléon*' peint par David, p. 41.

20. Ibid., p. 50.

21. Jean-François Boulart, *Mémoires militaires du général Baron Boulart sur les guerres de la République et de l'Empire* (Paris: Librairie illustrée, no date), p. 124.

22. Louis-Philippe de Ségur, *Extrait du cérémonial relatif au couronnement de Leurs Majestés impériales* (Paris: Imprimerie impériale, Frimaire An XIII (1804)), section III, p. 1.

23. Dubu, *Histoire, description et annales de la basilique de Notre – Dame de Paris*, p. 296..

24. Ibid., p. 292.

6. 1831 – HOW VICTOR HUGO'S NOVEL SAVED NOTRE-DAME

1. Reported in David Delpech, *La France de 1799 à 1848: entre tentations despotiques et aspirations libérales* (Paris: Armand Colin, 2014), p. 132.

2. Victor Hugo, *Notre-Dame de Paris*, tr. Alban Krailsheimer (Oxford: Oxford University Press, 1993), p. 119. All quotes from *Notre-Dame de Paris* in this chapter are taken from this edition.

3. According to Maurice Blanchot in 1943, and quoted by Adrien Goetz in his preface of Victor Hugo, *Notre-Dame de Paris* (Paris: Gallimard, 2009), p. 10.

4. Georges Duby, *The Age of the Cathedrals: Art and Society 980–1420*, tr. Eleanor Levieux and Barbara Thompson (London: Croom Helm, 1981), p. 166.

5. Ibid., p. 184.

7. 1844 – VIOLLET-LE-DUC

1. Viollet-le-Duc, letter to his father, 18 May 1835.

2. Françoise Bercé, *Viollet-le-Duc* (Paris: Patrimoine, 2013), p. 45.

3. Ibid., p. 51.

4. *La Correspondance Mérimée – Viollet-le-Duc*, ed. Françoise Bercé (Paris: CTHS, 2001), p. 53.

5. Eugène Viollet-le-Duc, *Entretiens sur l'architecture* (Paris: Librairies éditeurs, 1863), vol. I, p. 22.

6. Bercé, *Viollet-le-Duc*, p. 58.

7. Eugène Viollet-le-Duc, 'Peinture', in *Dictionnaire raisonné de l'architecture française du XIe au XVIe siècle* (Paris: A. Morel, 1864), vol. VII, pp. 56–109.

8. Bercé, *Viollet-le-Duc*, p. 94.

9. Ibid.

10. Ibid., p. 93.

11. Pierre-Antoine Gatier, interview with the author in Paris, 2 August 2019.

12. Eugène Viollet-le-Duc, 'Du style gothique au XIXe siècle', *Annales archéologiques*, 4, 1846, p. 352.

13. Philippe Villeneuve, interview with the author, 24 July 2019.

14. Rem Koolhaas, interview with the author from Rotterdam, 5 September 2019.

8. 1865 – HAUSSMANN 'UNCLUTTERS' THE ÎLE DE LA CITÉ

1. Pierre-Marie Auzas, *Les Grandes Heures de Notre-Dame de Paris* (Paris: Tel, 1951), p. 36.

2. Rupert Christiansen, *City of Light: The Reinvention of Paris* (London: Head of Zeus, 2018), p. 42.

3. Ibid., p. 49.

4. David P. Jordan, *Transforming Paris: The Life and Labors of Baron Haussmann* (New York: Free Press, 1995), pp. 199–202.

5. Pierre Nora (ed.), *Lieux de mémoire* (Paris: Gallimard, 1997), vol. III, p. 4206.

6. Pierre Gatier, architect-in-chief of Historic Monuments, interview with the author in Paris, 2 August 2019.

9. 1944 – DE GAULLE AT THE LIBERATION

1. Charles de Gaulle, *Mémoires de guerre II: l'unité 1942–1944* (Paris: Plon, 1956), p. 314.

2. Pierre Nora (ed.), *Lieux de mémoire* (Paris: Gallimard, 1997), vol. III, p. 4206.

3. According to Charles Glass, *Americans in Paris: Life and Death under Nazi Occupation 1940–1944* (London: HarperPress, 2009), p. 1. Nearly 30,000 Americans lived in and around Paris before the Second World War.

4. Ibid.

5. George F. Kennan, *Sketches from a Life* (New York: Pantheon, 1989), p. 74.

6. Pierre-Marie Auzas, *Les Grandes Heures de Notre-Dame de Paris* (Paris: Tel, 1951), pp. 37–8.

7. Agnès Poirier, *Left Bank, Art, Passion and the Rebirth of Paris 1940–50* (London: Bloomsbury, 2018), p. 66.

8. Editorial, *Combat*, 25 August 1944.

9. Yves Cazaux, *Journal secret de la libération* (Paris: Albin Michel, 1975), p. 184.

10. Now avenue du Général Leclerc.

11. Sartre's recollection, published in *Combat*, 2 September 1944.

12. De Gaulle, *Mémoires de guerre*, p. 290.

13. Ibid., p. 304.

14. Ibid.

15. Ibid., p. 306.

16. Audiovisual archives available at https://www.ina.fr/video/

I00012416/charles-de-gaulle-video.html (accessed 22 November 2019).

17. Ibid., p. 307.

18. Ibid., p. 308.

19. Ibid., p. 311.

20. Ibid.

21. Ibid.

22. Ibid.

23. Ibid., p. 313.

24. Interviews of witnesses to the events featured in *Soyez témoins*, a programme presented by André Gillois for France's national broadcaster on the assassination attempt against General de Gaulle on 26 August 1944. Broadcast on 26 January 1956. Available at https://www.ina.fr/audio/PHD89000578 (accessed 22 November 2019).

25. According to Raymond Marcillac, in his report available at https://www.ina.fr/audio/PHD86069770 (accessed 6 December 2019).

26. Ibid.

27. De Gaulle, *Mémoires de guerre*, p. 314.

28. Ibid., p. 321.

29. Ibid.

10. 2013 – THE BELLS OF NOTRE-DAME

1. The Parisian daily newspaper was founded in 1944; it had a circulation of almost 200,000 in 2018.

2. *Beaux Arts, hors série: Notre-Dame de Paris, telle qu'on ne la verra plus!*, 23 April 2019, p. 90.

3. Among the biggest donors were the Bettencourt family and the Sisley Foundation.

4. This one was made in the Netherlands and then sent to Villedieu-les-Poêles, where the other eight bells had been cast. They all departed together to Paris on 31 January.

5. Stéphane Mouton interviewed on *Racines et des ailes: les 850 ans de Notre-Dame*, France 3, March 2013.

6. Victor Hugo, *Notre-Dame de Paris*, tr. Alban Krailsheimer (Oxford: Oxford University Press, 1993), Book VII, Chapter 3, 'The Bells'.

7. Georges Duby, *The Age of the Cathedrals: Art and Society 980–1420*, tr. Eleanor Levieux and Barbara Thompson (London: Croom Helm, 1981), p. 95.

8. Ibid., p. 101.

9. André Chamson, Foreword, in *Notre-Dame de Paris 1163–1963: exposition du huitième centenaire organisée par la direction des Archives de France à la Sainte Chapelle, juin–octobre 1963*. (Paris: Direction des Archives de France, 1963).

10. Veronika Wand-Danielsson, interview with the author at the Swedish embassy in Paris, 23 July 2019.

11. About 100,000 euros.

11. 2019 – THE BATTLE FOR THE
RECONSTRUCTION OF NOTRE-DAME

1. President Macron during his second address to the nation about Notre-Dame, 16 April 2019.

2. Sybile Moulin, telephone interview with the author, 15 July 2019.

3. As he confided to Lorenzo Ciavarini Azzi in January 2019 in an interview available at https://www.francetvinfo.fr/culture/musique/classique/quot-bach-to-the-futurequot-l-039-organiste-olivier-latry-offre-bach-a-notre-dame-de-paris_3293749.html (accessed 25 November 2019).

4. As Olivier Latry confided to Alex Marshall from the *New York Times*. See 'Notre-Dame musicians rejoice that the cathedral's organ was spared', *New York Times*, 24 April 2019.

5. Jean-Claude Aillagon, email interview with the author, 22 July 2019. Mr Aillagon is François Pinault's spokesperson and was culture minister 2002–4.

6. Charitable donations in France normally benefit from a deduction against tax of more than sixty percent. The 'Notre-Dame Law' especially passed in summer 2019 raised this to seventy-five percent for every donation smaller than 1,000 euros given by individuals.

7. See 'Porch of Notre-Dame de Paris', Maisons Victor Hugo website, http://www.maisonsvictorhugo.paris.fr/en/work/porch-notre-dame-de-paris (accessed 25 November 2019).

8. *Le peuple est petit, mais il sera grand.*
   Dans tes bras sacrés, ô mère féconde,
   O liberté sainte au pas conquérant,
   Tu portes l'enfant qui porte le monde.

9. Jean-Claude Aillagon, email interview with the author, 22 July 2019.

10. According to the French public broadcaster France Info on 24 June 2019. See https://www.francetvinfo.fr/culture/patrimoine/incendie-de-notre-dame-de-paris/seulement-9-des-promesses-de-dons-pour-notre-dame-de-paris-ont-ete-versees_3488763.html (accessed 25 November 2019)

11. Monsignor de Sinety, interview with the author in his office, 11 July 2019.

12. In an interview with Vincent Remy, 'Notre puissance technique nous rend très vulnérables', *Télérama*, 24 April 2019.

13. Ibid.

14. Joris-Karl Huysmans, *La Cathédrale* (Paris: Tresse & Stock, 1898). *À peine jolie, mais si bizarre avec son sourire joyeux éclos sur de mélancoliques lèvres! Aperçue d'un certain côté, elle sourit à Jésus, presque railleuse. [. . .] Regardée d'un autre point, sous un autre angle, ce sourire, si prêt à s'épanouir s'efface. La bouche se contracte en une apparence de moue et prédit des pleurs. Peut-être qu'en parvenant à empreindre en même temps sur la face de Notre-Dame ces deux sentiments opposés, la quiétude et la crainte, le sculpteur a voulu lui faire traduire à la fois l'allégresse de la Nativité et la douleur prévue du Calvaire.*

15. All the following details are as told by Philippe Villeneuve in an interview with the author on the site of Notre-Dame cathedral, 24 July 2019.

16. Ibid.

17. Interview with Christine Ducros, 'Didier Durand, l'artisan devenu sauveur de Notre-Dame', *Le Figaro*, 24 July 2019.

18. Claire Bommelaer, 'Les Français opposés à une loi d'exception', *Le Figaro*, 9 May 2019.

19. Jacques Moulin, interview with the author at his office, 12 July 2019.

20. Ibid.

21. Father Gilles Drouin, interview with the author at Missions Etrangères de Paris, 2 August 2019.

22. Drawing on his experience there, Father Wresinski founded the International Movement ATD Fourth World.

23. Philippe Villeneuve, interview with the author at the cathedral's reconstruction site, 24 July 2019.

24. As he confided to Lorenzo Ciavarini Azzi in January 2019.

AFTERWORD

1. 'Chapuy and F.T. de Jolimont, *Vues pittoresques de la cathédrale de Paris et détails remarquables de ce monument* (Paris: Leblanc, 1823), p. 3.

Acknowledgements

Monday 15 April 2019 will remain a date to remember, not only because it was the night Notre-Dame de Paris came within thirty minutes of total destruction, but also because it was a moment of intense communion. From all over the world, I felt both the pain and the comfort of my friends and colleagues who instantly reached out: Allan Little was in California, Susan Clampitt in Washington, Shane Danielsen in Los Angeles, Simon Trewin, Farah Nayeri, Peter and Ilona Suschitzky, Nicolas Kent and Bill Swainson in London, Pedro Uriol in Madrid, Dominique Lempereur and Ion Babeanu in Hiroshima, Sophia Aram, Fiachra Gibbons and Pauline Dauvin across the Seine, and Benoît Cambillard on the phone again before dawn broke. Ken Loach texted the day after to say how affected he was. 'I was always moved to stand in Notre-Dame, so can only guess how you must feel,' he wrote.

The kindness of strangers is always as unexpected as it is moving: three days later, in Venice, a street-seller, on learning I was Parisian, came to me and said: 'When I saw her burning, I felt sick, sick to my stomach.' I would like to thank them all for their thoughtfulness.

This book wouldn't be as pertinent if it hadn't been for the time, kindness, help and knowledge of architects, art historians, writers, bakers, teachers, prelates, bee-keepers, ambassadors and generals. I would like to specially thank General Jean-Claude Gallet, Monsignor Benoist de Sinety, chief architects of Historic Monuments Philippe Villeneuve, Jacques Moulin, Marie-Hélène Didier and Pierre-Antoine Gatier, *cognoscenti* Philippe and Cécile de Cossé-Brissac, Father Gilles Drouin, author and climber Sylvain Tesson, art historian Adrien Goetz, bee-keeper Sybille Moulin, anthropologist Claudie Voisenat, *Madame l'ambassadeur* Veronika Wand-Danielsson and, last but not least, journalist and editor Jean-Dominique Merchet, and eagle -eye Linden Lawson.

Research was intense and I wouldn't have been able to cope without the enlightening words of the great medieval scholar Georges Duby and the music of Renaissance composer Giovanni Pierluigi de Palestrina, who accompanied me every day of this project.

One last special thought goes to François, Garance, Nicole, Henri-Louis and Jean-Noël who are always close. And to Angélique Chrisafis, who spent some precious time with me, watching Our Lady in flames.

Agnès Poirier, Paris, December 2019

Index